Armóred Hearts

Books by David Bottoms

POETRY

Armored Hearts: Selected and New Poems
Under the Vulture-Tree
In a U-Haul North of Damascus
Shooting Rats at the Bibb County Dump
Jamming with the Band at the VFW
    (*limited edition*)

NOVELS

Easter Weekend
Any Cold Jordan

ANTHOLOGY

The Morrow Anthology of Younger American Poets
    (*editor*)

David Bottoms

Armored Hearts

Selected and New Poems

COPPER CANYON PRESS

Publication of this book is supported by a grant from the National
Endowment for the Arts and a grant from the Lannan Foundation.
Additional support to Copper Canyon Press has been provided by the
Andrew W. Mellon Foundation, the Lila Wallace–Reader's Digest
Fund, and the Washington State Arts Commission. Copper Canyon
Press is in residence with Centrum at Fort Worden State Park.

Library of Congress Cataloging-in-Publication Data
Bottoms, David.
Armored hearts : selected and new poems / David Bottoms.
p. cm.
ISBN 1-55659-073-3. – ISBN 1-55659-072-5 (pbk.)
I. Title.
PS3552.O819A86   1995
811'.54 – DC20
95-6256

FIRST EDITION
0 9 8 7 6 5 4 3 2 1

COPPER CANYON PRESS
P.O. BOX 271, PORT TOWNSEND, WASHINGTON 98368

Grateful acknowledgement is made to the editors of the following magazines, in which all of the poems collected here first appeared: *The Atlantic, The New Yorker, Harper's, Poetry, The New Republic, The Paris Review, Antæus, The American Poetry Review, The Southern Review, The Kenyon Review, The Virginia Quarterly Review, America, Oxford Poetry (England), Ploughshares, Quarterly West, Crazy Horse, Iowa Review, Missouri Review, Black Warrior Review, Atlanta Magazine, New Virginia Review, The North American Review, Bennington Review, Mississippi Review, New Letters, Prairie Schooner, Southern Poetry Review, South Carolina Review, Southwest Review,* and *The Texas Quarterly.*

"Shooting Rats at the Bibb County Dump" and "The Drunk Hunters" first appeared in *Harper's.* "The Copperhead" and "Under the Vulture-Tree" first appeared in *The Atlantic.* "Under the Boathouse" and "White Shrouds" first appeared in *The New Yorker.* "The Tent Astronomer," "Last Nickel Ranch: Plains, Montana," "American Mystic," "Paper Route, Northwest Montana," "Sierra Bear," "Snake on the Etowah," and "Hard Easter," first appeared in *The Paris Review.* "Crawling Out at Parties," "The Catfish," "Watching Gators at Ray Boone's Reptile Farm," "Calling across Water at Lion Country Safari," "In a U-Haul North of Damascus," "Rest at the Mercy House," "A Home Buyer Watches the Moon," "Hurricane," "In the Wilderness Motel," "In the Black Camaro," "Rendezvous: Belle Glade," "Wakulla: Chasing the Gator's Eye," "The Drowned," "The Boy Shepherds' Simile," "A Tent Beside a River," "The Desk," "Naval Photograph: 25 October 1942: What the Hand May Be Saying," "The Anniversary," "Ice," "Appearances," "Homage to Lester Flatt," "The Guitar," "On the Willow Branch," "The Resurrection," "In Heritage Farms, Settled," "Rats at Allatoona," "Armored Hearts," "In a Kitchen, Late," "Cemetery Wings," "A Night, Near Berkeley Springs," "Home Maintenance," "Chinese Dragons," "Barriers," "The Pentecostal," "Warbler at Howell's Drive-In," "Horseshoes," "Home Buyer," "A Daughter's Fever," originally appeared in *Poetry,* copyright by the Modern Poetry Association.

"In a U-Haul North of Damascus" has been set into the symphonic song cycle, "Falling." Sincere thanks to Martin Bresnick, the composer.

The author gratefully acknowledges the support of the American Academy and Institute of Arts and Letters, the Ingram-Merrill Foundation, and the National Endowment for the Arts.

Thanks also to Maria Carvainis, James Dickey, Bob Hill, Andrew Hudgins, Charlie Smith, Dave Smith, and J. Stege, whose insight and kindness have been a constant support.

for Kelly and Rachel

It is hard sometimes to remember that beauty is another
word for reality.

— *Robert Penn Warren*

My soul is like a house, small for you to enter, but I pray
you to enlarge it. It is in ruins, but I ask you to remake it.
It contains much that you will not be pleased to see: this
I know and do not hide.

— *St. Augustine,* CONFESSIONS, *translated by*
R. S. Pine-Coffin

CONTENTS

I: *Shooting Rats at the Bibb County Dump* 1

Wrestling Angels 3
Smoking in an Open Grave 4
Shooting Rats at the Bibb County Dump 5
The Drunk Hunter 6
Below Freezing on Pinelog Mountain 7
Cockfight in a Loxahatchee Grove 8
Coasting Toward Midnight at the Southeastern Fair 9
A Trucker Drives Through His Lost Youth 10
A Trucker Breaks Down 11
The Farmers 12
Stumptown Attends the Picture Show 14
Jamming with the Band at the VFW 15
Writing on Napkins at the Sunshine Club 16
In Jimmy's Grill 17
The Hard Bargain 18
The Lame 19
Faith Healer Come to Rabun County 20
Crawling Out at Parties 22
The Catfish 23
Watching Gators at Ray Boone's Reptile Farm 24
Calling Across Water at Lion Country Safari 25
Rubbing the Faces of Angels 26

II: *In a U-Haul North of Damascus* 29

Rest at the Mercy House 31
Hiking Toward Laughing Gull Point 32
Neighbors, Throwing Knives 33
A Home Buyer Watches the Moon 34
Local Quarrels 35
Fog on Kennesaw 36
Recording the Spirit Voices 37
The Tent Astronomer 38

Sign for My Father, Who Stressed the Bunt 39
The Boy Shepherds' Simile 40
Sermon of the Fallen 41
Rendezvous: Belle Glade 42
Light of the Sacred Harp 44
In the Black Camaro 46
Under the Boathouse 48
The Christmas Rifle 50
Gigging on Allatoona 51
The Copperhead 52
The Fox 53
The Drowned 54
Wakulla: Chasing the Gator's Eye 55
In a Jon Boat During a Florida Dawn 56
Sounding Harvey Creek 57
In the Wilderness Motel 59
In a Pasture Under a Cradled Moon 61
In a U-Haul North of Damascus 63
Hurricane 66

III: *Under the Vulture-Tree* 69

In the Ice Pasture 71
White Shrouds 73
Ice 75
Red Swan 77
The Voice of Wives Dreaming 79
The Guitar 81
In Heritage Farms, Settled 82
The Resurrection 83
An Old Hymn for Ian Jenkins 85
Gospel Banjo: Homage to Little Roy Lewis 87
Homage to Lester Flatt 88
Face Jugs: Homage to Lanier Meaders 89
Awake 90
Gar 91
The Offering 92
Rats at Allatoona 93

Under the Vulture-Tree 94
On the Willow Branch 95
Fiddle Time 96
A Tent Beside a River 97
Shingling the New Roof 99
Appearances 100
Wings 101
The Window 103
In Louisiana 104
Naval Photograph: 25 October 1942: What the Hand May
     Be Saying 105
The Anniversary 106
The Desk 108

IV: *Armored Hearts 111*

Armored Hearts 113
Snake on the Etowah 114
In a Kitchen, Late 115
Cemetery Wings 116
American Mystic 117
Sierra Bear 118
A Night, Near Berkeley Springs 119
Home Maintenance 120
Warbler at Howell's Drive-In 121
Chinese Dragons 122
Barriers 123
Last Nickel Ranch: Plains, Montana 124
Paper Route, Northwest Montana 125
Hard Easter, Northwest Montana 126
Elegy for a Trapper 127
Last Supper in Montana 128
The Pentecostal 130
The Blue Mountains 131
Free Grace at Rose Hill 132
Zion Hill 133
Horseshoes 134
A Home Buyer 135

Sleepless Nights 136
A Daughter's Fever 137
Shelves on the Clark Fork 138
My Perfect Night 139
Allatoona Evening 140

1: SHOOTING RATS AT THE BIBB COUNTY DUMP

Wrestling Angels

With crowbars and drag chains
we walk tonight through a valley of tombs
where the only sounds are frogs in the reeds
and the river whispering at the foot of Rose Hill
that we have come to salvage from the dead.

Only the ironwork will bring us money,
ornamental sofas overlooking graves,
black-flowered fences planted in marble,
occasionally an urn or a bronze star.

But if there is time
we shatter the hourglasses,
slaughter lambs asleep on children's graves,
break the blades off stone scythes,
the marble strings on silent lyres.
Only the angels are here to stop us, and they have grown
too weak to wrestle.
We break their arms and leave them wingless,
leaning over graves like old men lamenting their age.

Smoking in an Open Grave

We bury ourselves to get high.
Huddled in this open crypt we lay the bottle, the lantern,
the papers, the bag on a marble slab,
tune the guitar to a mouth harp
and choir out the old spirituals.
When the shadows of this life have grown, I'll fly away.

Across Confederate Row an owl hoots our departure
and half-fallen brick becomes a porthole filled with stars.
We lay our ears against the clay wall,
at the foot of the hill the river whispers on its track.
It's a strange place where graves go,
so much of us already geared for the journey.

Shooting Rats at the Bibb County Dump

Loaded on beer and whiskey, we ride
to the dump in carloads
to turn our headlights across the wasted field,
freeze the startled eyes of rats against mounds of rubbish.

Shot in the head, they jump only once, lie still
like dead beer cans.
Shot in the gut or rump, they writhe and try to burrow
into garbage, hide in old truck tires,
rusty oil drums, cardboard boxes scattered across the
        mounds,
or else drag themselves on forelegs across our beams of light
toward the darkness at the edge of the dump.

It's the light they believe kills.
We drink and load again, let them crawl
for all they're worth into the darkness we're headed for.

The Drunk Hunter

Spun on a flat rock
his whiskey bottle points out magnetic north.
All afternoon trees stagger downhill
and up along ridges above thick brush.
He stops to watch them sway
and drinks the last of his Tennessee whiskey,
shoots the bottle off a pine stump.
Thinking there must be a logging road near,
he secretly hopes that someone heard his shot,
takes time to warn he's hunting posted land.

Come morning they will praise his patience,
tell stories in camp of a tree stand
frozen over a creek, how *old Jack never would come back
empty-handed*. In two or three days
they will tell what found him in the deeper woods.

Below Freezing on Pinelog Mountain

Crouched in the rusted cab of a junked pulpwood truck,
we take shelter from freezing rain,
count bullet holes shot in the hood by hunters.

Our burden is keeping dry
while dogs follow the game into darker woods,
white breath rising from their yelps like spirits
in that song land *where the soul never dies.*
But when you pass me the bottle,
cough for the whiskey burning
cold in your throat, that same breath fogs the windshield,
rises like gray smoke through rust holes in the roof.

Cockfight in a Loxahatchee Grove

Trucks backed against the canal,
we walk with our birds toward the depth of the grove
where the moon hangs hidden in leaves
and oranges bleed shadows across black dirt.

In lantern flare
they bolt and panic in their coops, gaze hawklike
at the circle of boots and Cuban feet.
Legs spurred like thorns,
their hearts throb toward rupture like ripe fruit.
In body shelter they are brushed and calmed.

Our circle widens like the pupil of an eye,
then lanterns are hung among oranges.
Flung toward light,
the birds jerk
the leather sheaths from their spurs,
collide between us in air and blood,
caw and heat. Crippled
and dragging wings, only one crawls back into our shadow.

Coasting Toward Midnight
at the Southeastern Fair

Stomach in my throat
I dive on rails and rise like an astronaut,
orbit this track like mercury sliding
around a crystal ball.
Below me a galaxy of green and blue neon
explodes from the midway to Industrial Boulevard,
and red taillights comet one after another
down the interstate toward Atlanta.

In the hot dog booth the Lions are sick of cotton candy.
Along the midway Hercules feels the weight of his
        profession,
Mother Dora sees no future
in her business,
the tattooed lady questions the reason
behind each symbol drawn indelibly beneath her flesh.

We all want to break our orbits,
float like a satellite gone wild in space,
run the risk of disintegration.
We all want to take our lives in our own hands
and hurl them out among the stars.

A Trucker Drives Through His Lost Youth

Years ago he drove a different route.
Hauling in a stripped-out Ford
the white hill whiskey nightclubs paid good money for,
he ran backroads from Ballground to Atlanta
with the cunning of a fox,
hung on each county's dirt curves like a banking hawk.

He remembers best how driving with no headlights
the black Ford felt for the road like a bat
and how his own eyes, groping at first for moonlight,
learned to cut through darkness like an owl's.
Sometimes he drove those black roads on instinct alone.

As the shadow of a bridge falls across his face,
his rear-view says he is not the same man.
Still tonight when there is no traffic, no patrol,
no streetlight to cast shadows or light the center line,
he will search again for the spirit
behind the eyes in his rear-view mirror.
Tonight in open country in heavenly darkness
the interstate to Atlanta will crumble into gravel and sand,
median and shoulder will fall into pine forest,
and his foot will floor the stripped-out Ford
till eighteen wheels roll, roll, roll
him backwards as far as his mind will haul.

A Trucker Breaks Down

Remembering himself pulling onto a highway
in Moultrie, Georgia, is remembering a direction, firm
    hands,
clear eyes. All roadsigns glowed in his headlights like true
evidence of things unseen. Only now have signs begun to lie,
become no more than compasses pointing degrees
for eyes that no longer believe in north.

So he dreams of breaking down between Moultrie and
    Savannah,
his truck rolling down a backroad alone
between barbed wire fences breaking into cotton fields
breaking into forest turning into pasture
where shadows graze under moonlight falling into deeper
    darkness,
always alone moving into the solitude of all nightmares,
becoming less and less a truck hauling freight,
becoming solvent, fluid, tires melting onto blacktop
crumbling into tar and sand, separating finally into currents
of water, becoming mist downstream, becoming fog
flowing down through absolute darkness into a pool of rising
    vapor.

The Farmers

Mouth full of wet bandanna bound
to the throat with a farmer's belt,
each wrist lashed to a length of rope,
they are leading you from the green field
to the barn, to a world of animals, up steps
to strap you across the hay-strewn floor.

One ties each wrist to the base of a rafter,
another shucks the shoes, the dress,
the panties, bra, binds an ankle
to an old anvil. The rope is gone.
They are feeling over you, new mounds
of white chest, fresh hair
that gleams like gold thread fallen
into the hay. They are kissing over you,
moaning over you, speaking to each wet breast
with a different tongue.
                              You can hear the snaps,
taste the belt that once held them silent
against a farmer's belly. Hands are holding
your free leg. You close your eyes, feel
thick fingers pointing the way to the womb.
You shiver in the ropes, try to listen
to the belly-heavy mare pacing in her stall,
the cluck and scratch of hens in the yard
anything but the thick breathing,
the live-leaving groans.
                              They swap positions.
A dog is at a cow's heels. Trucks begin
to growl in the distance. The mare is counting
time with her hoof. Crows are cawing
across the far fields. Snaps again.
                              One unties the leg,

the other a wrist. You open your eyes, struggle
with the other rope, watch them walk
down the steps, back to the fields and the reaping.

Stumptown Attends the Picture Show

on the first attempt at desegregation
in Canton, Georgia

Word has come and Martha the ticket girl
stands behind the candy counter
eating popcorn and smoking Salems.
Beside her the projectionist,
having canned Vivien Leigh
and come downstairs to watch the real show,
leans folding chairs against the theater doors,
guards his glass counter
like saloon keepers in his Westerns
guard the mirrors hung above their bars.

Outside, good old boys line the sidewalk,
string chain between parking meters
in front of the Canton Theater,
dig in like Rebs in a Kennesaw trench.
From the street, policemen and sheriff's deputies
address their threats to proper names,
try to maintain any stability.
Someone has already radioed the State Boys.

Through the glass door Martha watches
the moon slide over Jones Mercantile.
In front of Landers' Drugstore
a streetlight flickers like a magic lantern,
but Martha cannot follow the plot,
neither can the projectionist.
Only one thing is certain:
elements from different worlds are converging,
spinning toward confrontation,
and the State Boys are winding down some county road,
moving in a cloud of dust toward the theater marquee.

Jamming with the Band at the VFW

I played old Country and Western
then sat alone at a table near the bandstand,
smug in the purple light
that seemed like a bruised sun
going down over Roswell, Georgia.

A short bald man in a black string tie
and a woman with a red beehive
waltzed across the floor
like something out of Lawrence Welk,
his hips moving like a metronome in baggy pants,
her following like a mirror image.

For a long time I watched and drank beer,
listened to the tear-jerking music,
thought of all my written words,
all the English classes, the workshops,
the MA stored safely under my cowboy hat,
the arty sophisticates
who attend readings in Atlanta

and weighed against them
not one bald man waltzing a woman through another Blitz,
but all men turning gray who dream of having died
at Anzio, Midway, Guadalcanal.

Then rising from my chair
I drank the last of the Pabst
and moved through the bruised light of the bandstand
onto the purple dance floor, toward the tables
across the room, toward the table beside the bar,
and there the woman with platinum hair
and rhinestone earrings, moving suddenly toward me.

Writing on Napkins at the Sunshine Club

Macon, Georgia 1970

The Rock-O-La plays Country and Western
three for a quarter and nothing recorded since 1950.
A man with a heart
tattoo had a five dollar thing for Hank and Roy,
over and over the same tunes
till someone at the bar asked to hear a woman's voice.

All night long I've been sitting in this booth
watching beehives and tight skirts,
gold earrings glowing and fading in the turning light
of a Pabst Blue Ribbon sign,
beer guts going purple and yellow and orange
around the Big Red Man pinball machine.

All night a platinum blonde has brought beer
to the table,
asked if I'm writing love letters on the folded napkins,
and I've been unable to answer her
or find any true words to set down on the wrinkled paper.
What needs to be written is caught already
in Hank's lonesome wail,
the tattooed arm of the man who's all quarters,
the hollow ring and click of the tilted Red Man,
even the low belch of the brunette behind the flippers.

In Jimmy's Grill

The girl in blue-jean shorts
walks by our table and gives us the once-over,
eyes painted like we used to paint ours before ball games.
She stops at the jukebox, shifts her weight
to a stacked right heel, and the blue neon of a Budweiser
    sign
sparkles off the three rings in her ear.
She pushes buttons with deep red nails.

If it were only a matter of buying a few beers
or telling a lie about the money we made last year,
one of us would be asking if she has a sister.
But you only loosen your tie
and I point to the back of the room
where a beer gut rolls like a melon on the green pool table.

The Hard Bargain

In a pawnshop on Lucky Street an old Jew
sits in a wire cage, squints through thick bifocals,
and rolls a head smooth as a watch crystal
to check me in his convex mirror.

What I have brought is something from long ago.
He makes his offer and I shop
for a decision among the clutter of his shelves,
measure his degree of profit among old war medals,
watch chains, empty frames that once held pictures
of people who hocked their whole lives
piece by piece in a series of bum deals.
But there's no sense in holding out. The guitars
strung across his wall, the radios and portable TV's,
earrings and bracelets, wedding bands in his glass counter
all say he drives a hard bargain.

The Lame

Dragging the foot to the water's edge
the boy waits, watches the man in rolled shirtsleeves
raise and lower the waterlogged Bible,
then steps into the red current,
dreams he feels fish gnaw the swollen ankle,
carry off in their bellies chunks of his deformity.

They meet in the middle of the river.
Kneeling at the healer's feet, water to his shoulder,
the boy listens   *a certain man lame from his mother's womb*
and at command rises, walks back across the current
fluidly toward land, toward his family's anxious eyes,
Mama with her basket of fried chicken, Daddy
with the family Bible, and scattered across the bank
the wondering eyes of the healed and afflicted all focused
on the river's edge, watching for the promise to emerge.

When the twisted foot breaks light, flops across sand
like a dying fish, mama closes the basket, daddy the book.
All the whole and newly healed leave the river lame.

Faith Healer Come to Rabun County

Seldom is that tent full, but tonight he expects the local
    radio
to draw a crowd, also the posters up for weeks
in barbershop windows, beauty parlors, convenience
    groceries.
Even now his boys are setting out extra folding chairs,
adjusting the P.A. for more volume, less distortion,
wheeling the piano down the ramp of a U-Haul trailer.

In the back of a red Ford van he goes over his notes
on the healing power of faith:
the woman of Canaan whose daughter was rid of a devil,
the lunatic healed who fell no longer into fires,
the Sabbath healing of the withered hand,
the spitting into the eyes of the blind man of Bethsaida
who first saw men walk as trees
and then after the laying on of hands, men as men
walking on legs among those trees.

Even now he can smell the sweat, the sawdust,
the reviving salts,
feel the healing hysteria
run electrically through charged hands,
hear the quivering lips babble into the piano music.
Who would be healed, he will say, must file to God's altar
and stand in awe at the laying on of hands,
or those unable to be in the congregation
need only lay a hand on the radio,
withered as that hand may be it will be whole.

And if all goes as he prays it will go
even the most feeble will quake down the sawdust aisle,
kneel or fall unconscious at his shocking touch
to rise strong, young, healed in the spirit.
There is medicine in the passionate heart, he will say,

there is medicine in the power of God's love.
O Jesus, Savior, touch this sick brother
who accepts in faith the things we cannot know,
O sisters come to the altar, lay your hands on the radio.

Crawling Out at Parties

My old reptile loves the Scotch,
the way it drugs the cells that keep him caged
in the ancient swamps of the brain.
He likes crawling out at parties
among tight-skirted girls. He takes
the gold glitter of earrings
for small yellow birds wading in shallow water,
the swish of nyloned legs for muskrats in the reeds.

But he moves awkwardly in the hardwood forests
of early American furniture, stumbles on grassy
throw rugs, and the yellow birds
flutter toward the foggy horizons of the room.
Out of date, he just can't swing
so slides back always to his antique home,
the stagnant, sobering water.

The Catfish

From a traffic jam on St. Simons bridge
I watched a fisherman break down his rod,
take bait-bucket in hand, and throw
to the pavement a catfish too small to keep.
As he walked to his car at the end of the bridge,
the fish jumped like a crippled frog, stopped
and sucked hard, straining to gill air.
Mud gathered on the belly. Sun dried the scaleless back.

I took a beach towel from the back seat
and opened the car door, walked to the curb
where the catfish swimming on the sidewalk
lay like a document on evolution.
I picked it up in the towel
and watched the quiver of its pre-crawling,
felt whiskers groping in the darkness of the alien light
then threw it high above the concrete railing
back to the current of our breathable past.

Watching Gators at Ray Boone's Reptile Farm

While we stand behind the concrete railing
and yellow cockatoos cry through mosquito heat,
the gators never move,
but look like floating logs almost ready to sink,
wait as though long patience had taught them something
about humans,
an old voice crying up from the swamps of our brain.

Once that cry called a small boy
over the railing and the logs came alive.
A black man in a Bush hat salvaged the legs.
On the bottom of the pool
Ray Boone found a shrunken white hand clutching a stone.

Our hands clutch concrete as we lean against the railing
as though leaning might bring us closer
to that voice crying now through our common memory,
the answer to all the animal inside us.

Calling Across Water at Lion Country Safari

Across Reptile Pond a herd of zebra graze in open green
captivity, black-striped necks bent to bales of hay
dropped by natives from truck beds.
An ostrich trots into the herd
and a few colts break toward a tree by the green canal
where a giraffe neck thin as straw
needles the leaves of lower branches.

On Ape Island a gibbon moves like a gray blur
through the limbs of a leafless tree.
Below him two chimps leaning on their knuckles
watch our cars roll by in procession
something like a line of elephants in a circus.
In the back seat our Safari guide
speaks through the taped drumbeats of a darker continent,
warns against leaving cars or throwing food.

But a silverback gorilla in the mouth of a cave
sees my lens spark against the sunlight.
His hairy arm stretching slowly toward the car
curls back to his chest.
My shutter catches his eye,
the long talking arm circling in and out, calling me
across water, the only thing he believes is really between us.

Rubbing the Faces of Angels

I:

On the balcony of the Golden Eagle Motor Inn
a black maid pushes a linen cart.
Businessmen pass on the sidewalk below,
heels clicking like nickels on the pavement.
As she takes a key from her waist chain
and enters a darkened room,

a gray-haired man in a green turtleneck ambles down the
        steps
of the Gibbes Art Gallery
fighting the wind for his copy of the Post.
Reaching the street
he turns toward the Mills Hyatt House
where a black doorman in tophat and tails
carries luggage across a red carpet and into the lobby.

Up and down Meeting Street people are resuming routines,
but for me this is a new city and year,
a few hours to gather fresh images
while you labor across the street
in the graveyard of the Circular Congregational Church
writing in your notebook small records of the dead,
with charcoal and rice paper
rubbing the faces of angels from stones.

2:

At Western Sizzler you tell me death
on the oldest stones
is a hollow-eyed skull,
sometimes over crossbones, other times wings
(later skulls grew detail,
evolved into the faces of angels),

and describe how the skull
cradled in bones
above the grave of David Stoddard
became the skull and wings of Desire Peronneau,
became the angel frowning over Elizabeth Mathews,
the angel rejoicing over John Gerley's grave.

After all this time, you say,
we are coming to judge death less critically.

3:

The gray-haired man
is asleep in a house on some Charleston street.
Tomorrow he will walk up the same steps.
Businessmen in shiny suits will pass again
under the balcony of the Golden Eagle.
The black maid will roll her cart above their heads,
look from her balcony and watch
people from other cities, countries,
rub the same stones you rubbed today,
take photographs,
record the same sparse data of the same spent lives.
All over Charleston
things will move routinely toward one fact.

Yes, after all this time
we are coming to judge death less critically.

Even you and I
taping these rubbings
to the wall of Howard Johnson's Motor Lodge
point to this one and that
and say we'd like the figure carved on our stone,
you a smiling angel, wings curled toward heaven,
me the reclining skeleton of Thomas Pool.

II: In a U-Haul North of Damascus

Rest at the Mercy House

Because nature doesn't specialize
in mercy, this House of Refuge was raised behind the dunes
on Gilbert's Bar,
provisioned with fuel and blankets, cereals
and dried meat, for the survivors of ships wrecked
on offshore reefs. And in its time
adequate to its vision.

Now with others
we parade behind the hatchery and marvel
how the newborn turtles cobble the bottom of their tank,
wander past aquariums of native fish,
tap our fingers against the glass, little codes
we want them to know us by, then tread
the boardwalk down to the beach
where survivors in another time waded
toward shore with whatever they could salvage,
mostly themselves.
                    No more shipwrecks
off this coast, only a few survivors of wrecked
or uncharted lives, a few tourists
looking for a place to beach. Across the dunes
the sea oats wash back and forth in a gold froth.
Gulls and black skimmers, pelicans and terns,
take sanctuary in the weathered hollows of the sea wall.
Here nothing is molested, all blest.
For travelers like us, a tour of the house, a vision,
a momentary rest.

Hiking Toward Laughing Gull Point

Once I saw a gull catch a bait in midair.
Climbing until the slack ran out,
it snapped back like a white feather on the end of a whip
and fell into the sea.

We've all swallowed a line or two,
a real estate deal, some bad investment of faith, or so
I tell myself as I walk
past the fishermen casting their cut shrimp on the water,
the overweight women wading in the surf,
the tower where the boy lifeguard hangs against the blue sky
and dreams behind his sunglasses a dream of salvation.

As I near the same sandy point I hike toward every year,
stand at the edge of the wing-
flutter, my white skin burning red, the sun bleaching
what's left of my hair, I think how the point
keeps drifting farther away
like some water-mirage
or a piece of land in a speculator's dream.
How each summer I search for my dream
vacation, only to find myself feeling more like some gull
climbing toward the edge of an island,
a hook, the end of the line.

Neighbors, Throwing Knives

In the woods at the corner of our yards
we hang the plywood squares,
the Magic Marker images of pronghorn, panther,
grizzly, whitetail,
and step off the paces we use to measure
our skill.
        Here in the soft light filtering
through needles and cones, green shifting
membrane of poplar, hickory, live oak,
white skin of dogwood beginning
to flower, we heft the blades,
grind points on stone, gauge the fine balance
between what is real and what is imagined,
the knives bringing all the animals to life
and killing them again
as our throws bury steel deep in the heart
of the quivering wood and the blades tremble
back through their bones.
        In our own hearts
we love what they might be, their shapes
frozen in brush as though, suddenly,
they had turned from wood
and caught our scent drifting in a wind-shift.
So we hunt this suburb, whet our aim
to move among them in the little wilderness
beyond the bricked-in beds of azaleas,
sunflowers tied against tall sticks,
the half-acres of razored grass,
trellised vines, boxwoods manicured by wives.

A Home Buyer Watches the Moon

The whole neighborhood is quiet.
The architect who lives across the street
is now the architect of dreams, his cedar split-level
still as a crypt on the landscaped hill.
In the brick ranch house
the city planner turns another spadeful of dirt,
a groundbreaking for his own monument. And I,
who can no longer afford to live
in my two-story, have come out into the street
to stare past the mailboxes at an abrupt dead end.

Quietly now the bats jerk
in and out of the streetlight, their shadows
zipping across the grass like black snakes.
And the moon lies balanced on the roof of my house
like a new gold coin, or the simple face
of an angel in a Colonial cemetery.

Local Quarrels

As though the nineteenth century hadn't crumbled
and polite society still made pretensions
about honor, we left the party boozing in the house,
and half walking, half staggering,
followed our principals across the backyard
and gas-lamped garden,
the barbed-wire fence, the pasture spotted with ponds.

All around us oak branches trembled,
and far across the field of ponds and black mounds
of cattle sleeping in clusters in the cool dew,
we could see against a dark horizon of pines
the light that was the house.

Face to face they stood in the full-moonlight
surrounding them with shadows,
arms at their sides, and began on signal
to step in opposite directions, looking straight ahead
as we all counted with our hearts
the twelve quick paces before they turned
and the long pistol-cracks spread through the pasture.
Heads cocked in sudden amazement,
they listened as the shots faded and one cow lowed
and waded into water. When neither fell
they sat in a common shadow.

Fog on Kennesaw

We pitch our tent on Kennesaw Mountain,
pull the hemp rope tight, set the steel stakes,
lean our pick and shovels against the trees
like the rifles of Joe Johnston's army.
On the south side of the mountain,
we are hidden from the park rangers, clothed
in the brush like the ghosts of Loring's Rebels.

Nothing has changed here but the century.
These same neutral stars
saw Rebels shoot rocks from cannons.
Trees along these slopes and fields hold rifle balls
in their healed-over bark.
                              At sunrise
we will patrol Little Kennesaw for minié balls and bayonets,
scour the woods where McPherson drove his Yankees
into the eyeballs of French's cannons. But tonight
we have found something seeping up through the leaf-
        cover,
the pine straw, something drifting across old earthworks,
maneuvering on Kennesaw.

Recording the Spirit Voices

In the hollow below the hill vaults
I have placed a recorder
on the grave of a young woman killed in a fire
and have crouched under the arm of this angel
to wait for voices,
tree frogs whirring through the blue pines,
the Ocmulgee lapping the bank at the foot of Rose Hill.

A gray moon over the Confederate graves
gleams on the water,
the white gallon jugs floating some man's trotline.
Like me, he's trying to bring things to the surface
where they don't belong.

And across the river
blue needles rasp like the voices
I heard on television,
the documented whisper of spirits, *I'm afraid here, I'm
      afraid.*
So am I now
as leaves in the hollow rustle their dry tongues:
afraid to hear a woman scream from a burning house,
to record some evidence her tombstone lied,
bury the truth these angels stand on: *born* and *died.*

The Tent Astronomer

As a barrier against mosquitoes,
I pull an old sheet from the closet,
then cross the yard,
enter the field bordering the orange grove
where the sleeping bag lies behind the low tripod,
the hammer and stakes wait in the damp grass.

At each corner
one stake goes into the sandy ground,
then the sheet stretched over the four points,
pulled down and anchored with stones.
The darkness underneath is private.

I lie still for a while
and listen to cicadas crying by the canal,
the crickets and barking toads,
stinkbugs breaking against the walls like small clods,
then with my knife
cut a hole for the barrel,
let lens and mirror lift me up toward light.

Sign for My Father, Who Stressed the Bunt

On the rough diamond,
the hand-cut field below the dog lot and barn,
we rehearsed the strict technique
of bunting. I watched from the infield,
the mound, the backstop
as your left hand climbed the bat, your legs
and shoulders squared toward the pitcher.
You could drop it like a seed
down either base line. I admired your style,
but not enough to take my eyes off the bank
that served as our center-field fence.

Years passed, three leagues of organized ball,
no few lives. I could homer
into the garden beyond the bank,
into the left-field lot of Carmichael Motors,
and still you stressed the same technique,
the crouch and spring, the lead arm absorbing
just enough impact. That whole tiresome pitch
about basics never changing,
and I never learned what you were laying down.

Like a hand brushed across the bill of a cap,
let this be the sign
I'm getting a grip on the sacrifice.

The Boy Shepherds' Simile

Wind rose cold under our robes, and straw blew loose
from the stable roof.
We loved the cow tied to the oak, her breath rising
in the black air, and the two goats trucked
from the Snelling farm, the gray dog shaking with age
and weather.
                    Over our scene a great star hung
its light, and we could see in the bleached night
a crowd of overcoats peopling the chairs.
A coat of black ice glazed the street.

This was not a child or a king,
but Mary Sosebee's Christmas doll of a year ago.
We knelt in that knowledge on the wide front lawn
of the First Baptist Church
while flashbulbs went off all around us
and a choir of angels caroled from their risers.
This was not a child wrapped in the straw
and the ragged sheet, but since believing was an easy thing
we believed it was like a child,
a king who lived in the stories we were told.
For this we shivered in adoration. We bore the cold.

Sermon of the Fallen

From an east window
a screen of light sliced across the walnut box.
I sat and watched the grain rise dark,
and listened to him tell
how muscles wither under the skin,
and the skin dries and flakes away from the bone
like gray bark flaking from the trunk of a fallen pine,
how the forest trembles once as the tree falls
and somewhere a bird whimpers from a ridge,
then nothing,
and what needles are left yellow-green
and clinging to limbs
shimmer a few times in the rain, then lose
all color and drop away,
and the gray pine shines through the bark like bone,
cracks and sours, softens with larva,
collapses in shadow, belches gas
from its grainy soup, dries
in sun to a black forest dust, then seeps
with rain through the pine-needle floor.
So, he said, you had come to fall.
Even as a boy, I could feel the trembling in us all.

Rendezvous: Belle Glade

Pine thicket at the edge of a clearing:
I squatted with my back against a tree
and cradled in my lap the Enfield carbine,
a pawnshop gun, not terribly accurate,
but terrible and accurate enough,
a jungle weapon designed for use in Burma.
Under black branches I knew were green
as money, I hefted its weight,
checked night vision through peep sight
and saw over the dull gleam
of the cone-shaped flash suppressor
the field where Florida sand boiled up
like smoke and fireflies snapped off
against the far border of trees.
Inside those trees a truck sat under a canopy
of low branches, and around that canopy
Cubans hid and listened for a voice
on the two-way radio.
                              I listened for an owl
to call again from the pines dissolving
into glades behind me, for the voices
of tree frogs to blur toward a monkey-laugh
riddling the trees of Burma, for wind
to crackle like brush under boots,
and felt in my heart a weakness like malaria,
which I knew was only the shaking
of nerves, like the tips of my fingers
caressing the scars on the Enfield,
tracing crude letters of the one deep scar
that was the name the soldier Lowry
had carved into his stock.
                              From the sky
came the first sign, a far-off, insect drone
of an engine buzzing the dark above
the southern horizon, then a burst of light

stringing the edges of the field
and the airstrip glowing in the forest
like a flesh wound. I found my hands close
around the rifle as the droning grew loud
and twin props swept tree-level and were gone,
leaving only a wake in the pinetops
and a blown field of wrapped bales hitting
between the strands of light
and rolling in the sand like paratroops.
In the darkness of snuffed lanterns,
I stood in a silence awaiting all-clear,
wondered what I might do if a floodlight
of the law should jar from the trees.
I tapped the magazine, thought of Lowry
killed and buried in Burma,
or alive, perhaps, with family in England,
his retirement and his life closing in,
and how on other nights
he sat listening in the jungle for Japs,
how silence made him as jumpy as noise
and nerves edged a name in his stock.

Light of the Sacred Harp

Small fire of hymnals in a trash can,
the spirit of shape-notes rising in smoke
as we huddle at the altar, watch
our song-cloud hover under the ceiling,
rise through a broken window
into the cold dark. Here we share
in the good new warmth of God's old house
the warmth of the bottle carried through woods
and field. Here we drink the new wine,
the plasma of visionaries and hunters,
until the spirit of that blood moves
in us, moves in the legs
of the offering table, the swayed backs
of pews, the splintered crosses bearing panes
of wavy glass, dark faces frowning
from the table of the Last Supper, staring
through the ashes of our hymn-words
floating up like dust on fire, floating up
and vanishing like the yelps of our dogs
vanishing in the trees beyond the field
of stumps, the tombstones
weedy with briars, the collapsed steps,
the jimmied door.
                        As though this were a light
to see all things by, the fire draws us
into its vision, a choir of voices rising
behind the crackling music, a clapping
of sweaty hands, swaying of bodies
in a hot night, the slap of rhythm sticks,
tambourines, bottle caps rattling
in a hollow gourd. And we chunk in hymnals,
funeral home fans of the Sermon on the Mount,
Jesus in the wilderness, Jesus at the door,
chunk in a bouquet of dead flowers
to watch the fire jump around the pulpit

like something catching spirit, hear
old voices burning back from the graveyard
in newfound harmony as the pulpit catches
and becomes light, and we kneel
for drunkenness and joy as fire climbs the wall
and enters the Last Supper, the air filling up
with psalm-smoke, the whole house of the Lord
popping with revival, becoming pure spirit
of voices returning in the joyful noise
of the Sacred Harp, singing over and over
the good gospel news that men do rise from dust
and ashes.

In the Black Camaro

Through the orange glow of taillights,
I crossed the dirt road, entered
the half-mile of darkness and owl screech,
tangled briar and fallen trunk, followed
the yellow beam of Billy Parker's flashlight
down the slick needle-hill,
half crawling, half sliding and kicking
for footholds, tearing up whole handfuls
of scrub brush and leaf mold
until I jumped the mud bank, walked
the ankle-deep creek,
the last patch of pine, the gully,
and knelt at the highway stretching
in front of Billy Parker's house,
spotted the black Chevy Camaro parked
under a maple not fifty feet
from the window where Billy Parker rocked
in and out of view,
studying in the bad light of a table lamp
the fine print of his Allstate policy.
I cut the flashlight, checked up
and down the highway. Behind me
the screech growing distant, fading
into woods, but coming on
a network of tree frogs signaling
along the creek. Only that, and the quiet
of my heels coming down on asphalt
as I crossed the two-lane and stood
at the weedy edge of Billy Parker's yard,
stood in the lamp glare of the living room
where plans were being made to make me rich
and thought of a boat and Johnson outboard,
of all the lures on a K-Mart wall,
of reels and graphite rods, coolers
of beer, weedy banks of dark fishy rivers,

and of Billy Parker rocking in his chair,
studying his coverage, his bank account,
his layoff at Lockheed, his wife laboring
in the maternity ward
of the Cobb General Hospital. For all
of this, I crouched in the shadows
of fender and maple, popped the door
on the Camaro, and found
in the faint house-light drifting
through the passenger's window
the stripped wires hanging below the dash.
I took the driver's seat, kicked
the clutch, then eased again
as I remembered the glove box
and the pint of Seagram's Billy Parker
had not broken the seal on. Like an alarm
the tree frogs went off in the woods.
I drank until they hushed
and I could hear through cricket chatter
the rockers on Billy Parker's chair
grinding ridges into his living room floor,
worry working on him like hard time.
Then a wind working in river grass,
a red current slicing
around stumps and river snags, a boat-drift
pulling against an anchor
as I swayed in the seat of the black Camaro,
grappled for the wires
hanging in darkness between my knees,
saw through the tinted windshield
by a sudden white moon
rolling out of the clouds, a riverbank
two counties away, a place to jump and roll
on the soft shoulder of the gravel road,
a truck in a thicket a half-mile downstream.

Under the Boathouse

Out of my clothes, I ran past the boathouse
to the edge of the dock
and stood before the naked silence of the lake,
on the drive behind me, my wife
rattling keys, calling for help with the grill,
the groceries wedged into the trunk.
Near the tail end of her voice, I sprang
from the homemade board, bent body
like a hinge, and speared the surface,
cut through water I would not open my eyes in,
to hear the junked depth pop in both ears
as my right hand dug into silt and mud,
my left clawed around a pain.
In a fog of rust I opened my eyes to see
what had me, and couldn't but knew
the fire in my hand and the weight of the thing
holding me under, knew the shock of all
things caught by the unknown
as I kicked off the bottom like a frog,
my limbs doing fearfully strange strokes,
lungs collapsed in a confusion of bubbles,
all air rising back to its element.
I flailed after it, rose toward the bubbles
breaking on light, then felt down my arm
a tug running from a taut line.
Halfway between the bottom of the lake
and the bottom of the sky, I hung like a buoy
on a short rope, an effigy
flown in an underwater parade,
and imagined myself hanging there forever,
a curiosity among fishes, a bait hanging up
instead of down. In the lung-ache,
in the loud pulsing of temples, what gave first
was something in my head, a burst
of colors like the blind see, and I saw

against the surface a shadow like an angel
quivering in a dead-man's float,
then a shower of plastic knives and forks
spilling past me in the lightened water, a can
of barbequed beans, a bottle of A.1., napkins
drifting down like white leaves,
heavenly litter from the world I struggled toward.
What gave then was something on the other end,
and my hand rose on its own and touched my face.
Into the splintered light under the boathouse,
the loved, suffocating air hovering over the lake,
the cry of my wife leaning dangerously
over the dock, empty grocery bags at her feet,
I bobbed with a hook through the palm of my hand.

The Christmas Rifle

Over the spine of the ridge
orange light scatters through pine and briar,
sifts into the gorge.
With the red glove of his right hand
my father points toward a branch near the top of a pine,
raises the sawed-off stock to my shoulder, lifts
the barrel and backs away.

The gray squirrel moves in front of the sun,
and light shoots down the barrel like a ricochet,
turns blued steel silver from bead to sight.
He points again
and I follow the dark green sleeve of his jacket
to his red outstretched finger
to the squirrel crouched in the fork where the branch
joins the trunk.

Don't jerk. Don't pull. And I watch that spot of air
where the gray squirrel jumps,
then drops from limb to limb in stiff gymnastics
until it strikes the ground at the foot of the pine.
I cradle the rifle and walk to the squirrel, prod
the soft belly with the barrel, study
the hole over the left shoulder, the fine gray hair,
white near the roots, puffed out around a circle of blood.
Just behind me, my father is walking on needles,
the weight of his hand comes down on my shoulder.

Gigging on Allatoona

Light bleeding onto pines
and pine shadows crawling across water turning orange
under boathouses floating under an orange sky,
we huddle on a ruined dock, file barbs sharp,
load buckets with ice and beer, wait
for the chorus of lake-edge croaking.

Darkness fallen, we shove off
onto the water, pull ourselves along the beams
our flashlights anchor to the bank
toward the bass-throb belching in the starless night,
the voice that dies as we drift toward a rustle
in the cove-grass, the cattails waving.
And when the light finds the bulging slime eyes,
we feel the thrust and jab, the tilt
and rock, the small twitch of legs
kicking air at the end of the gig, the wake
rolling away from the boat far out across the black water.

The Copperhead

A dwarfed limb
or a fist-thick vine, he lay stretched
across a dead oak fallen into the water.
I saw him when I cast my lure
toward a cluster of stumps near the half-buried trunk,
then pulled the boat to the edge of the limbs.
One ripple ran up his back like the tail
of a wake,
and he lay still again, dark and patterned,
large on years of frogs and rats.

I worked the lure around the brush,
oak and poplar stumps rising out of the water
like the ruins of an old pier,
and watched his spade head shift on the dry bark.
But no bass struck
so I laid the rod across the floor of the boat,
sat for a long time watching the shadows
make him a part of the tree,
and wanted more than once to drift into the shaded water,
pull myself down a fallen branch toward the trunk
where he lay quiet and dangerous and unafraid,
all spine and nerve.

The Fox

A quest brought a gray fox to the field behind my house.
In a circle of dirt
where drought had starved away the grass, he fell
to one knee, rubbed an ear on the ground
as though he were listening for heat to crack the field.

I snapped a clip into the handle of the Beretta
and stepped off the porch.

The slamming of the screen froze him. He stood up
and spread his legs for balance, shook a bright red halo
of dust around his head, and wandered toward me,
legs out of sync, mouth oozing saliva and mud.

He sidled along the edge of the field where tomato vines
fenced my yard, then struck a crooked path
between the stakes, tangled, and tripped to one shoulder.
The powdery soil rose around him like waves of heat.

I sat in a lawn chair and watched him wallow in exhaustion,
his dull, matted throat pulsing for quick breath.

Then nosing the air and the ground, the tomato leaves
and the dwarfed tomatoes, he caught a scent,
jerked his shoulders through vines and string,
staggered out of the tomato garden and into the yard

where what he needed to find moved in the blur
of the azalea bush and the guava tree, the lawn chair
and the long brown yard stretching toward the gray house.

The Drowned

Arms finned-out across the water,
he floated face down in the crotch of a fallen oak.
I cut the outboard
and rode the current, paddle-steered
toward the water stilled in the limbs of the tree.

In the bend where the river pooled and deepened,
my stomach jumped like something caught
and I pulled up short,
waited for breath, let my eyes follow water downstream
where the string of plastic milk jugs
floating my trotline
bobbed like heads on the surface of the river.

Then I drew the boat closer,
watched the slack of his blue jeans roll in my wake,
his head nod gently against the thick oak branch,
long hair tangled in the branch-twigs.
I eased the paddle out and touched his heel.
He didn't turn or move, only gazed straight down
into the deepest part of the Etowah
as though fascinated by something I couldn't see.

Wakulla: Chasing the Gator's Eye

If you catch a gleam between pad stalks
or a gleam among river trash bogged in the scum of algae,
cut the outboard and drift,
fix your spotlight on the eye's red shining.

Through the dark it will come to you
like a reflector on the edge of a dock
where there is nothing like a dock,
only pads and algae, and the endless drift of the Wakulla
washing slowly under.
                          Ease toward it on that drift,
your light fixed on the eye's bright circle.
And if you approach as a part of this river, give over
to your truest self, something
washed down like all things washed toward the gulf,
the reflector may hold on the surface of the river,
and you can see in its deep red shining
the reptile that moves beneath you.

In a Jon Boat During a Florida Dawn

Sunlight displaces stars
and on the Wakulla
long cypress shadows streak water burning
light and clear. If you look around you,
as you must, you see the bank dividing itself
into lights and darks, black waterbugs
stirring around algae beds, watermarks circling
gray trunks of cypress and oak,
a cypress knee fading under a darker moccasin,
silver tips of river grass breaking
through lighted water, silver backs of mullet
streaking waves of river grass.
For now, there are no real colors, only tones
promising change, a sense
of something developing, and no matter
how many times you have been here,
in this boat or another,
you feel an old surprise surfacing
in and around you. If you could,
you would cut the outboard
and stop it all right here at the gray height
of that anticipation. You would hide yourself
in this moment, cling to an oak branch
or a river snag
and stop even the slightest drift of the current.
In fresh sunlight distinguishing loggerhead
from stump, moss from stone,
you would give yourself completely
to the holding,
like the lizard clinging to the reed cover
or the red tick anchored in the pit of your knee.

Sounding Harvey Creek

I:

Under the narrow, splintering, slatted floor of the dock,
a snake glides toward the clear shallows,
his head a dry leaf riding the surface,
his back a band of hourglasses, hazel and chestnut.
Over the floor of broken shells,
schools of tiny, unseineable minnows dart from his course
and close again as he slides into reeds,
quiver in his wake like slivers of orange light.

I unfold the legs of my chair,
sit and face the water, the mud turtles helmeting snags
and stumps, two mallards skiing the neck of the creek,
green heads bobbing.
Across the pine-bristled back of Squirrel Island,
a heron drags its snaky throat.
Nothing looks more alien to the sky, yellow legs
hanging like sticks. I must seem at least that strange,
my wrist whipping air with a switch of black graphite.

2:

I concede my ignorance of fishing,
the stringer coiled
in the bottom of my tackle box, my dull
and virginal Eagle Claws,
my impotent wealth of jitterbugs,
doll flies, Mirr-O-Lures,
spoons that glow like jewelry
in their plastic boxes.

What I love about water is mystery,
the something unknowable
curling under roots, the thing lost

sinking with each current
deeper into sludge,
the obscurity of depth
and the infinite variety of oddities
crawling out of that depth
to reveal nothing: frog and stinkpot,
waterdog fanning red gills,
the mole salamander, the common newt,
the dwarf siren, the copperhead
burdening the reeds
with a beautiful danger.

And the hours of awesome ignorance –
enough possibility to make me reel.

3 :

In the styrofoam bucket, the shiners
fall through my fingers like jewels. Across the wide mouth
of Harvey Creek, nothing stirs in the wooded yards
of retirement homes, the screens still dark in their shades,
the outboards locked in their boathouses.
Nothing stirs in the black pinetops
feathered with crows.
                                  In the reeds behind me
the copperhead waits with the patience of a stick,
and in the middle of the creek
opening into Lake Talquin, the water turkeys perch
on the jagged backs of protruding limbs,
motionless above the turtles. I listen for absolute silence
in the unsoundable depth of all water.

A pale bait catches light in my hand.

Is it wrong not to love the transparency of minnows,
their bones showing like veins in a tiny leaf?

In the Wilderness Motel

1:

Red star hovering
over the tip of the half-moon, and we follow
the blacktop through fenced and unfenced pasture,
fields of okra
and beans and corn, past
hog farms and shanties, mobile homes scattered
in clusters of shade oak
until we reach the horseshoe drive,
the gravel parking lot
under the burnt-out neon of the Talquin Motel.

Here the weeds have moved in
for good, rat and coon are regular guests.
Pines root away the concrete walls, drop their limbs
across the roof, and all night
the wind sweeps the rooms,
blows old garbage into different corners.

Where the last reservations are layers of mold
on a plywood desk,
we come to fill a vacancy.

2:

Once in Valdosta
the phone rang and we thought we were found out.
It was only a recording, an advertisement
for the Red Fox Lounge,
an extended happy hour with live music.

But that whole evening
we heard voices,
people we knew or thought we knew

singing above the guitar, the electric bass throbbing
through the floor, through the walls
of our uneasy privacy. And into the night,
their laughter rising like rumors around the pool,
their shadows crossing the curtains,
car doors slamming in the parking lot.

3:

Around the edge of the dry pool,
beer cans rust in a mulch of needles and leaves,
candy wrappers, paper cups, newspaper
blackened and turning back to pulp. Someone has rocked
the bulbs in the pool lights, splintered
the diving board against the drain. The only music left
is the trees, the wind
cutting high notes over reeds of broken glass.

We sit on a warped deck chair
and watch the cosmic balancing, the red star sliding down
the edge of the moon, the wilderness sliding
across the face of this abandoned motel. Somewhere
in all these wrecked rooms, there is a darkness we can slide
into, a shredded mattress that will ease us into love
and sleep.
                    And when we wake
in the caked layers of leaf-rot, blown-dirt,
burnt-sheet, we can listen through the shattered window
for the raccoon digging in the trash, the grating
of claws on concrete, the owl,
the cicada, the tree frog. We can celebrate
the comfort, the company of ruin.

In a Pasture Under a Cradled Moon

1:

Hung between pinetops
three stars cradle the moon. Below, on a sliced hill
where the moss-webs of live oak hang over the roofs
of chicken houses, the chicken wire
of a dog lot leans over the gorge of the new road.
Crouched behind that wire, a dog
barks at the great yellow roundness of the moon.

I listen from this field of stumps,
watch the black cattle
fold their legs, roll full-bellied on the wet ground.
Salt blocks grow like new teeth
around the lip of the pond. Wind combs
the ragged Johnson weed, wrinkles the skin of the water.
And I think how the moonlight falls
or doesn't through the window beyond the field,
the pond, the wall of pines,
falls or doesn't on the bed where you sleep.

2:

What might have been
is like a vague throat-pulse croaking from a cove-shade
or the gargle of bass striking frog spawn, a sound
almost clarifying, like a murmur
from the field's edge, the wing-purr
of horseflies swarming over dung.

Or else like an image
almost solidifying, a cloud of fireflies swarming
between the poplars near the pond, one creature
almost becoming whole, molecular,
but dissolving with the quickness of light.

3:

Only a quiet now.
A quiet chorus of frogs, a leg-beat
of crickets, a distant, muffled grinding of a diesel
gearing for a long incline.
And the long black shadows of poplar and pine
streak the field, blossom
with the black hulks of cattle, the charred clusters
of burnt stumps. Between the pinetops
the yellow roundness of the moon
falls through the cup of stars, and I remember how
in the half-hour before sunrise
you cramped and doubled, small blood
spotting the bedsheet, and then a deluge,
the future miscarried.

Wind crackles in the high branches,
rains dry leaves into the field,
onto the backs of cattle rolled against the fences.
And in the room where you rest, the ferns
nod from the dresser, the Wandering Jew quivers
from the window basket to the floor, sheet and blanket
curl around your shoulder. I will sit here
only a while longer
studying the way the light drops into the trees,
the way so much love can be learned
from loss.

In a U-Haul North of Damascus

Lord, what are the sins
I have tried to leave behind me? The bad checks,
the workless days, the Scotch bottles thrown across the fence
and into the woods, the cruelty of silence,
the cruelty of lies, the jealousy,
the indifference?

What are these on the scale of sin
or failure
that they should follow me through the streets of Columbus,
the moon-streaked fields between Benevolence
and Cuthbert where dwarfed cotton sparkles like pearls
on the shoulders of the road? What are these
that they should find me half-lost,
sick and sleepless
behind the wheel of this U-Haul truck parked in a field on
	Georgia 45
a few miles north of Damascus,
some makeshift rest stop for eighteen wheelers
where the long white arms of oaks slap across trailers
and headlights glare all night through a wall of pines?

2:

What was I thinking, Lord?
That for once I'd be in the driver's seat, a firm grip
on direction?

So the jon boat muscled up the ramp,
the Johnson outboard, the bent frame of the wrecked Harley
chained for so long to the back fence,
the scarred desk, the bookcases and books,
the mattress and box springs,

63

a broken turntable, a Pioneer amp, a pair
of three-way speakers, everything mine
I intended to keep. Everything else abandon.

But on the road from one state
to another, what is left behind nags back through the
        distance,
a last word rising to a scream, a salad bowl
shattering against a kitchen cabinet, china barbs
spiking my heel, blood trailed across the cream linoleum
like the bedsheet that morning long ago
just before I watched the future miscarried.

Jesus, could the irony be
that suffering forms a stronger bond than love?

3:

Now the sun
streaks the windshield with yellow and orange, heavy beads
of light drawing highways in the dew-cover.
I roll down the window and breathe the pine-air,
the after-scent of rain, and the far-off smell
of asphalt and diesel fumes.

But mostly pine and rain
as though the world really could be clean again.

Somewhere behind me,
miles behind me on a two-lane that streaks across
west Georgia, light is falling
through the windows of my half-empty house.
Lord, why am I thinking about this? And why should I care
so long after everything has fallen
to pain that the woman sleeping there should be sleeping
        alone?
Could I be just another sinner who needs to be blinded

before he can see? Lord, is it possible to fall
toward grace? Could I be moved
to believe in new beginnings? Could I be moved?

Hurricane

1:

At twilight
the leaves of palmettos screeching like cicadas,
orange limbs rustling around green oranges,
oleanders whining toward the west.
Over the edge of the field,
the pinetops breaking like white water, and the first rain
squalling in from the sea, peppering hollow
on the storm awnings,
washing down the latticed door.

At the church site across the field, animation
and rapture,
lumber scraps rising out of the dirt like Baptists
at the Second Coming. Over the tractor shed
a swirl of shingles, gray wings
beating into the grove, lodging in branches
or rising into the pines across the road.

As long as the gray light holds under the clouds
we stand at the door
and watch how the wind breathes a special life
into everything not tied down.

2:

And when the drenched light dies, we sit
in candlelight
and listen to the voice on the radio static,
north-northwest, twelve miles an hour,
and the repeated cautions of fallen wires, bad water,
the deceptive calm of the eye
and the wind that whirls back without warning.

What whirls now are shadows
as the candle flickers from the ledge above the cabinet
and the kitchen falls black,
the wind bombing the house with oranges, whistling
under the storm awnings rattling against the walls.

And we wonder if the roof will hold, wonder
until the shot cracks behind us
and a window shatters from a church-stud driven
through an awning, wind exploding the room in glass
    shrapnel
as we fall from our chairs, in time or not,
to shield our faces from the slivers, to find a door
and close it behind us, give the kitchen up
to the storm.

3:

Light gathers
behind a glass door,
and a scrub lizard crawls down the screen.
The oleanders lean back toward the ocean.
Bark peeled and strewn,
the melaleuca shakes broken limbs toward the sun.

We cross the grass blown dry in the gales,
walk rows of orange trees and kick the fallen fruit,
piece together a picture of the damage,
a wrecked kitchen, a shed wall collapsed and blown away,
a few lines downed by limbs. Not so much.
Even the half-moon scabbing above my eye
is a good sign, something to be glad for. The way
the quail whistles its reprieve from the saw grass
across the road,
the ox beetle gores up through blown sand.

III: UNDER THE VULTURE-TREE

In the Ice Pasture

Something cried in the field and I took the binoculars
into the yard, the zeroing wind,
saw in what starlight the glasses gathered
the gray barn, the empty pasture haunted
with trees, nothing.
And then in patches the deep prints
tracking the hill, the snow trail floating
over the broken fence
where the horse walked fifty yards onto the pond
to fall neck-deep through the ice.

What was he trying to become out there,
thrashing to get a hoof up
like an odd beast cracking his shell?

I ran to the basement for an ax
and out the basement door, outrunning my breath
to the edge of the bank,
where he calmed to watch me tap with the handle,
creep three-legged onto the pond,
as though he wanted me to witness the beauty
of his change – only a quiver of the head
as he waited,
half a white statue in a fountain of ice.

Sleet, like static, crackled the pond
as I eased him back from the blade of the ax.
Then behind me a noise like the snapping of bones
and my feet stood on nothing as I grabbed
for his mane, sank chest-deep
in the shock of the cold,
both of us sinking, hooves
pounding legs, kicking me under.

How long did I hang there, numb,
bodiless, before the body of the horse rose under me
and what we were lunged hard, broke
to the air, to the wind turning us scaly
with water?

The sleet blistered the pond, the ice groaned.
Then the first kick. And the hacking, the snorting,
till the roar we made broke up the dark
in the throats of dogs, the cattle bedded
in the field, broke by inches the black shell
of water, till the night
cracked like an egg shattered in the storm
of two beasts becoming one,
or one beast being born.

White Shrouds

From our kitchen window I watched the hard sleet chipping
at the granite pond, the white ducks
huddling in their giant mushroom, and felt against
my leg the warmth in the heater vent die.

Did you feel how cold it dropped that night?

At nine below, water expands into rock, the pipes peel
back like ripe fruit,
the heavy branches of the post oak bang like axes
against the house. The power fails
all over the neighborhood,
the ferns on the windowsill crack like china.

I went down to the basement to check the firewood,
wormy, maybe enough for one night,
then pulled the couch in front of a fireplace
too shallow for any real heat, wrapped you in a skin
of quilts, let you tuck and sleep
inside what comfort it gave.
                                    On the end of the couch,
outside the eye and breath of the fire, ice
actually crusted the tips of my beard.
And in that other place where the cold takes you
out of yourself with each white breath,
I listened to the fanatical ministry
of the brain, the alarm
it sounds to keep the body alert,

which wasn't the ringing of bells over city shelters,
or the sirens of ambulances spinning out of alleys,
but was only that breathing,
the white easy breathing of sleepers curling

in doorways, behind dumpsters, their ears
slowly turning into stone, and no one
to husband the small logs, two at a time, onto the fire.

Ice

No one this far south chances ice.
So what was I to think when I sat down for breakfast
on the morning after Christmas
and saw through our glazed kitchen window
the whole pond frozen white,
and out of the stiff gray pines on the far side
of the pond, our neighbor's teenage daughter
edging down the bank
one careful step at a time, a boot on a rock,
a boot on a ledge? She stopped at the lip of the ice,
picked up a rock large as a brick
and threw it out, watched it chip the surface
and slide. Then holding to a pine branch,
put down a foot and tried her weight.
I ran slow as a glacier,
or seemed to, as I pushed from the table,
and when she let go and shuffled away
from the bank, what could I do
but stand on my deck and shout the warning
that froze in the breath between us?
In the middle of the pond, all around her
water turned into something strange,
she began, of all things,
to shift on one leg, then the other,
each step sure as a prophecy,
each foot kicking thunder into the heads
of fish. Then up on her toes,
one leg sweeping her into a spin, arms flung out,
mittens like a blue dream circling her head.
And when she heard me and spun to a dizzy stop,
saw me in my ragged underwear,
barefoot on my deck,
when her hands came down to lift the hem
of an imaginary skirt
and she curtsied and turned and walked away,

I remembered a story her father told of growing up
poor in small-town Ohio,
how every year in the hard of winter
the mayor drove a rattletrap onto the river
and the lottery began.

Red Swan

Purple necks and green, fat drakes whiter than Easter
live on our five acres of suburban water
with one gray goose, a Canadian honker
who came a year ago and settled.
And occasionally other birds, locally exotic,
drop by the lake, a few gulls, an egret,
and once a wood ibis, all the thrill
of the neighborhood kids
coaxing them to stay with bread crumbs.
We know why these birds come to us, little stops
on ancient journeys, but the strangest of all
came straight from the blue, parcel post,
a prank gift or a mistake. One evening
we came home and found the box on the porch,
no return address. Inside was a plastic night-lamp.
orange bill, red body, pink feet,
gaudy, out of place anywhere in the house.

I unscrewed a bulb from a table lamp,
screwed it into the grassy base, plugged the cord
into an outlet, and cut the overhead.
Then in our living room something
out of science fiction! And possessed
we stared till that light sank in
and showed us the brilliance
of the thing we were determined to do.

We pulled the extension cords from the typewriter
and the television, from the electric fan
cornered on the side porch,
took from the basement the fifty-foot cord
uncoupled from the weed-eater, dragged them all
into the backyard, where the sky leaned
black and defiant, strung them end on end
from the rear deck socket all the way to the edge

of the lake, propped the lamp
in the tall grass by the shallows.
On that water it burned like a returning god!
Not long then before the great goose, being
called, honked out into the cove,
the ducks breaking huddle on the bank,
dogs barking awake behind their fences,
until one by one in the houses around the lake
the upstairs windows lit up like eyes.

That goose still honks on the lake, all night,
haunted. And in the stories
of the neighborhood kids,
the ibis is commonplace, the snowy egret nothing
to speak of. There is only that sighting
too beautiful to believe, quick
and radiant as revelation,
and all their stories tell of a night
when lightning waddled down to the edge of the lake
to burn for a moment in the shape of a swan.

The Voice of Wives Dreaming

Some nights I wake to the cry of the child
who drowned in our pond,
and I crawl from my bed, dress,
leave my wife in her drift of sleep,
walk into the yard, down to the bank
where the water holds as many stars
as the sky. And if I ponder drifting out
onto that black heaven, if my arms
quiver like wings, I only stand
by the lip of the water and listen
for the voice disappearing,
the voice disappeared, the water.
And if the brush rattles I'm not startled.
I say, *Yes, it's happening again,*
and the vines crawling the oak limbs
rustle like a curtain as my neighbor walks
into the moon, points toward the far bank,
the thicket of pines, the flashlights
of other neighbors divining water.
We meet them again by the earth dam
and give the hard testimony,
who first saw the body blooming white
as a lily in the oak roots,
who untangled the grassy drifts of hair,
who pried the fingers from the ball
of the sun. And repeat our stories
of other mornings, the eyes of our women
startled out of sleep, their hands still
shaky at the table, spilling coffee,
the frightful talk. So long ago now
you'd think we might lose a thing
like a flower under the knee of an oak,
but in the women the current moves
another way. Or so we account for it
as we back into the woods, onto

the trails along the bank, knowing
in this we account for nothing,
can only gather, listen, witness,
then stagger off, wakeful,
toward our own backyards, the deck lights
edging the doorways we enter
to find again that communal drift of sleep
where each woman floats face down
dreaming the voice of a different child.

The Guitar

Alone on a hill above the festival, I listen past field noise
to the single bird note humming
off the prongs of a metal fork, and twist the keys
of my guitar, flat, then sharper, trying to pull
all loose tension into line, to rest each bronze string
on the one clean level of sound all musicians strive for.

Then across the hill walks a fiddler coming from another
      jam,
his bow pointing me out in the dark, his fiddle
fluttering under his chin, "Bill Cheatum"
already bridging the distance between us.

How long before his ear, pitched to those bright true notes,
brings to his face the blank disappointment of the moon,
and he saws the tune short,
walks off toward the field, the notes rising like sparks
around the campfires?

And these nights when you come home late from work
or whatever, highstrung
and restless, and already turned in
I'm a case of insomnia, each sorry fret buzzing in my head,
or if by chance asleep, awakened
by your little torches of sound, the low opera
of a late night movie, the click of your lighter –

how long do I lie in that room, waiting for a footfall,
the bright run of bracelets,
wondering how a night could be as wide as a field,
and why, when you lie down beside me, both of us silent,
I wonder again at the guitar, how anything studied so long
could suddenly go strange in my hand?

In Heritage Farms, Settled

In their tennis whites, their pastel Izods, all day the women
walk down my street, their Coppertoned children
sleek as seals, trailing to the courts
and the pool.

Through my wall of loose screen I watch the neighborhood,
the mowers, the gardeners, the crew
of movers wrestling with a van of Early American.

What worries me most is this constant settling,
my dog refusing to bark at joggers, content to stalk
to the edge of the porch, whimper back
to his nap, his muscular breathing.

Sometimes without warning, gravity seems to surge,
the house trembles and the foundation sinks
a little deeper into the lawn.
Then the Volvos crawl through the street, and neighbors
read a month of mail beside their boxes, water
the same pink rose for hours.

This is when I force myself into the yard,
when I blow through the woods bordering the pond,
kicking whole colonies of mushrooms, the stinkhorns,
the devil's urns, when I make tracks and look for tracks,
following the creek with its cargo
of debris, desperate for something to praise,

something small and changing,
the delicate white maggot wagging in its cradle
of turds, the tiny feet of the tadpole, every leg
of the hornworm inching toward the wings of the phoenix
    moth.

The Resurrection

I'd dared her to go in, and we came on that dare
to the road above Rose Hill Cemetery,
and sat for a moment in the cab of my truck,
quiet, not talking, looking down
at the valley of stones, the bone-white
testaments prickling the hills.
All the way out she'd talked of death, her desire
to be cremated, have her ashes scattered
over Lake Rabun. In the new life she'd return
as a swan or a dove. What did I say?
That I believe in the new life too,
the resurrection of the body, and though I knew
the Lord could mend us ash by ash
I wasn't the sort to put Him to the trouble.
So I wasn't afraid, we were as different
as East and West, and the night was still cool,
not quite the season to fall in love
with the wrong woman. And if she was afraid
of anything, she didn't show it, only
took the flashlight off the seat, zipped her parka.
A bright half-moon, white as marble, hung
over the river, and I followed her
in that light as she edged through the trees
down the hill toward the gardens,
toward the creek, the row of bricked vaults.
I'd dared her to go in. Not into the graveyard,
but into a grave I knew lay open in the side
of a ridge, an old haunt, reputed hangout
of a witches' coven. And I wasn't afraid
until I stopped where the rock garden
bridges the creek, and the wind off the river
seemed the breath of the dead, or whatever
inside me was dying. *Let's go*, she said,
and pointed up the ridge where I had pointed
to the grave, and we followed the creek

up the valley past the wrought-iron fences
and chairs, the patios and bedrooms
of the dead, without talking, without touching
or ever having touched, until we came
to the end of the valley, the black mouth
gaping behind branches. She knelt then
by the tree and shined the light –
wine bottles, a sardine can, stubs of iron bars
jagging those jaws with rusty teeth –
and with only a slight shiver against the cold,
we crawled into that belly of earth.
What had I really expected to find? A pit
of beer cans, a clay chamber of dry roots?
Or that stir in the sudden falling of dark,
like the brush of a cobweb against an ear,
like the silky crawl of the first hungry worm,
the gentlest touch,
that first delicate laying on of hands?

An Old Hymn for Ian Jenkins

All things we value in terms of contrast,
the Ian Jenkins walking tour of New York
taught me that. Chelsea, the Bowery,
Little Italy, the long track
across Chinatown, my round eyes opening
to the light of the immigrant East.
And in the Garden of the Golden Dragon,
you dissecting my displacement,
punctuating with the click of chopsticks
the Jenkins theory of urban alienation.
That analogy of the hive dweller,
his drone-like problems with identity,
that whole argument for territory,
sinks in now with the sunlight raining
through the gaps in these trees.
And as we cross the field from the house
to the pond, still groggy from the Mets
game, the late miles on the turnpike,
I know why you and the Upper West Side
zip to these mountains on weekends.
Last night, through the dead black
of time, a horse snorted in the woods,
a carriage rocked down the wheel ruts
of the road and stopped in front
of the house. Downstairs the front door
slapped closed, and cards fluttered
like wings across tables, all I remember
of the house showing my sleep the past.
And what it neglected of the grounds,
the field where the local militia drilled
for the Revolution, the Colonial graveyard
at the foot of the hill, you fill in,
from landmark to landmark, piecing time
and dirt like the rags of history's quilt.
I understand that. Southerners know

how a place can wrap you up in a dream.
And what this place puts me in mind of,
the clear river edging the green field,
the solid house beyond the graves,
are the elements of an old hymn,
Flatt and Scruggs wide open on your stereo,
their mansion over the hilltop, their land
of beautiful flowers where we'll never
grow old. What I'm talking about
is that place we go to save ourselves,
that place in the dream where the object
of the dream is place.

Gospel Banjo:
Homage to Little Roy Lewis

Three days I lay with a fire under my skin, in the guest room,
in the twin bed by the window.
The preacher in waist-high water, his Bible, the walnut
        frame,
the footboard, everything
shimmied in heat, the lights mostly down,
the brightest thing in the room
the banjo cracking in the speakers of the stereo.

That last night I fell into a dream of a river, a cold wind
brushing my arms straight out
toward the gray water, open and deep, too wide to see across.
And anchored on that bank, a little white boat
wormy with scars.
Little Roy, can you imagine that long drift,
the tenuous ark of the dream
like a single note sailing farther and farther from the string?

All I remember is waking under the full moon floating
in the window,
the shell of your Mastertone swimming in a tablature of
        stars.

Little Roy, to come back to anything as clear and bright
as your banjo, to watch the stars
wink off every note,

to roll toward the room and hear each riff spark
across the distance,
and to ease back, cool and clear-headed,
alive and listening,
is to hear the dream flaunting the possibility of the dream,
which is the joy of waking on either side of the Jordan.

Homage to Lester Flatt

Troublesome waters I'm fearing no more

Five seasons without traveling to a festival, without walking
into a field and hearing that voice.

And now after a long spell of rain, I step off my porch
and walk toward the river,
remembering the last time I saw Lester Flatt,
how thin he looked and sick
as he sat back in a lawn chair under the sagging pines
of Lavonia, Georgia,
and scribbled his name on the jackets of records.

How do the roots chord, Lester?
And the click beetle and the cricket, the cicada, the toad,
what harmonies do they sing in the high grass?

All of those voices
want me to praise your remarkable voice –

Tonight little sparks are winking in the fields, and the dead
are combing the edge of the forest, their arms
full of campfires.
Tonight the dead are building a stage under a funeral tent
and blowing the dust off banjos.
Tonight, for you, the dead are shaking the worms
from their ears.

Lester, singing whatever we want to about the dead
is the easiest thing in the world.
Believing it the hardest.
So this is where I stop, in this wet grass.
This is the river we're all troubled by, where the storm wash
rattling the bank echoes the tenor of our lives.

Face Jugs: Homage to Lanier Meaders

From the tailgate of a pickup on the shoulder of Georgia 52,
from the crafts tent at the White County Fair,
the right face may find you,

or from the wall of the mountain store at Tallulah Gorge,
one face shelved among his many brothers,
the pig-face, the devil-face, the moon-face, may turn
just the right way in the light
in the leaves, in the light tinted by gingham, by walls
of doll clothes and pastel quilts, may turn
to you, his eyes stunned awake by the knowledge
that yours is the face he was meant for.

There is nothing to do then but lift him from the shelf,
nothing to do but hold him
by the window where the light from the wavy pane
makes a mirror of his glaze, your eyes
swimming in his gouged sockets, your cleft on his chin,
your lips floating over his tongue.

You hear again what that tongue is fired to say, the old
admonishment, the clay and the flesh.
But he is simply you, and as you walk to the car,
happy as a man who's found his puzzle's missing piece,
it frightens you to think you might have left him.

And when you get home to the city,
when you move the crystal cherub into the dining room
and place the fern on the mantle, when you
polish the end table and ease him down on slick mahogany,
all you feel is gratitude. And you relax on the sofa,
smiling at the melon head, the pancake cheeks,
the yellow, rock-toothed mouth grinning back in deep relief.

Awake

A winter so hard you think the shrubs may never rouse,
the redtips stunned in their brown coma,
the boxwoods flaking like pillows of rust.
Then one day, weeks late,
the first bud winks on the China tree,
and the maple sapling, leafless,
sends a green tentative feeler
into the yard. Underground
something is stirring, climbing through the veins.

That night the shadows leave a warmth in the air,
a promising stillness,
so you take your rod and tackle box,
you walk the quarter mile of thickening woods,
stand in the weedy mire bordering the shallows,
ease your fly onto the surface.

And you see in what light the stars give the lake
a wavy V zagging the water, a spade head
running the brush shadows, vanishing,
and the water smoothing to a plate of black glass.
The wind blows the honeysuckle
out of the pines, and the surface ripples easy
with the drift of twigs and feathers.
The old needles alert the new leaves,
the fly jitters under a bush.
A gray breath of fog yawns out of the cove
and the tail washes up on your boot.

Gar

All night the river house swayed
on stilts, and mosquitos navigated the slit screen to find me
asleep on the top bunk and salty with sweat.
From a dream of fish
their kisses stung me into the stifling heat
and the steam rising off the river,
and I rose dazed and found my clothes,
my line and my tackle.

A red sun bobbed into the rushes
and pricked the skin of the river, long needles of blood
stabbing the bank where a ribbon snake slipped
off a root and into the water, where a skink climbed
a brown stone, where my reel whined
at the river thrashing under the rush shadows, a rusty snout,
a saw blade from the old world, hacking
like a memory at the light.

The Offering

Into the scrap pine I jerked the saw, guessing dimensions,
leaving the edges rough, and tacked the boards
into a feeder,
two simple shelves like open hands.
Where the willow hangs over the pond
I propped my ladder and hung
my shelves in the top of that tree, poured
the mixed seeds of five grasses.

Before any birds trusted enough to come
days passed, then together came blackbirds and sparrows.
For hours I gave myself
to the catbirds and jays, the mockingbirds
who caught in their throats the voices
of all the neighborhood beasts, known and unknown.

Eventually not even their songs were enough.
Where was the voice they couldn't mimic?

Now at night I wait on my porch, anxious
with my tiny guilt, and rock
back in my chair, watching
through binoculars the dark jaw of pinetops,
the trees on the edge of the pond, the willow trembling
under the feeder,
where the dead mouse lies in the starlight,
white as a soul, fat as a tongue.

Rats at Allatoona

Over the lake the stars scatter their crumbs of light,
shadows skirt the pines, the docks
treading the cove,
and through those shadows rats ease toward the campsites,
the metal drums rich with the garbage
of weekenders.
                    I listen, drunk, on this deck
as their feet fill up the dark. Above the crickets
and the soft lap of water,
they pray a squeaky grace of fine nails climbing
the rusty sides of cans.

Tonight I'm dreaming of walking out toward them,
of stumbling over rocks
toward the cove, blind as a shadow, homing
on their rapture. Tonight
my dream is to lie down among them
and feel on my neck in the boozy wave of sleep
a first whisker, a moist nose,
the needle comb of a paw, and to stir in sunlight
in the wet grass
of the cove, among cans
and ashes, shreds of their sacrament,
and finger my hair and my face,
wake to what I am in my dream
and my body, whole
and broken, having taken from the feast
and given to it, the tip of a thumb,
the lobe of an ear.

Under the Vulture-Tree

We have all seen them circling pastures,
have looked up from the mouth of a barn, a pine clearing,
the fences of our own backyards, and have stood
amazed by the one slow wing beat, the endless dihedral
    drift.
But I had never seen so many so close, hundreds,
every limb of the dead oak feathered black,

and I cut the engine, let the river grab the jon boat
and pull it toward the tree.
The black leaves shined, the pink fruit blossomed
red, ugly as a human heart.
Then, as I passed under their dream, I saw for the first time
its soft countenance, the raw fleshy jowls
wrinkled and generous, like the faces of the very old
who have grown to empathize with everything.

And I drifted away from them, slow, on the pull of the river,
reluctant, looking back at their roost,
calling them what I'd never called them, what they are,
those dwarfed transfiguring angels,
who flock to the side of the poisoned fox, the mud turtle
crushed on the shoulder of the road,
who pray over the leaf-graves of the anonymous lost,
with mercy enough to consume us all and give us wings.

On the Willow Branch

Now the pond is still and the softest paddle stroke eases
the boat into the cove. Over the floating stars
you drift, the water settles around you.

The eyes widen as the body remembers,
the stars flare over the pines.
Down cove the tree frogs line their favorite hymns
and the wood drake listens.
At your fingertips the water strider performs
his nightly miracle.

Then a branch above the jon boat rustles like breath
and you look up. Nothing,
then the rustle again, and you shine the light.

Red eyes spark on the willow leaves,
flare, selfless,
and suddenly you're ashamed of your loneliness.

The wind gusts hard on the pond, and the branch sways
out of your beam. The jon boat tosses
easy in the wave-slap, and the old brain clings
to the spine.

Fiddle Time

Off the fiddle of a man who rented a garage from my father
came the first music
I remember hearing. His name is lost and his face,
but I remember the sparrows nesting
in his rafters, and the boxes of shatterproof auto glass,
the rolls of vinyl and cloth, the heavy Singer
for stitching seat covers.
                              And how seldom he did
any upholstery business or worried about that business
as he leaned over his plywood bench
in sunlight edging through gaps where sheets of red tin
hung loose or rusted away from the roof,
sanding for hours the swell of a close-grained face,
the taper of a neck, an *f*-hole.

And I remember clearly those Sunday afternoons, his bow
sparking rosin off the fiddle strings,
the strained face of the guitar player, a beat behind,
a beat ahead, though I can't recall one tune they played,
not a snatch of a melody.
                              The truth is
he wasn't that smooth a fiddler. But he cared
for the fiddle, and in the memory's raw first music
I still catch a measure of that care,
a jigsaw blade, a gruff file humming,
or the sandpaper rasping in the tips of his fingers
as he shuffles time,
not quite lost, over the curve of a finely honed bridge.

A Tent Beside a River

Remembering lanterned, canvas-sprawled fields
of the county, we gathered for dream's sake
under the roof of the blue nylon tent,
opened Bible and Baptist hymnal
under a flashlight's yellow stain
to call into play our own miracle. And afraid
we'd be found out of bed, sang in whispers
the few songs we could sing, to be heard
only by the One we wanted to hear.
Then I, who could read best, read what
I could from the Scripture, my breath
the rustle of leaves over a lip of open water.
For in the house at the yard's heart,
our grandfather lay dreaming of Jordan,
his face gone pale as the light shining
through his curtained window, a lamp
they would not turn off, as though it kept
him from crossing by anchoring his shadow
beside him. For an hour in the yard
choirs of crickets echoed hymns
and short winds chorded the trees.
Then far off in the tall dark of pines
beyond the house, an owl with a voice deeper
than time announced the lateness of the hour.
We were new at grief, and weak,
and let ourselves fall toward sleep,
forgot the house and the lamp, the old man
wrestling his shadow. But this is not
entirely true. When the tent flap snared
the dark, a light came on behind our eyes
and each of us saw him a special way.
Then the owl came down to find us, whistled
a note of departure, and we remembered,
real or not, a shadow drifting over the roof.
They found us, too, in morning light, huddled

in a ball like a litter of strays,
and rousted us with voices nervy and crisp
as the air, as though children
had never dreamed of such,
nor their words ferried anyone safely anywhere.

Shingling the New Roof

On the roof of the garage my father was hammering into a
     house,
I tacked on shingles with the men,
carried nails up and down the ladder, and made a wage.

Four of us up there among the limbs that kept the sun
off one whole side of the house,
our neighbor, my father, and my grandfather
whose house it was to become. Four of us finishing the roof,

and my mother sending up Cokes and sandwiches
in a bucket strung over a limb. My mother telling me to
     watch
my step, to stay away from the ledge, telling my father
I was too small to be on the roof.
                              And maybe I was,
but I didn't think so, even when I jerked too hard
on a stubborn nail and tumbled, hammer-loose,
in a backward somersault, feet upside down into the air
above the yard, hands just hooking the gutter.

I remember my body dangling fifteen feet above the spikes
of the picket fence,
and my father's face, whiter than caulk, as he scrambled
toward the ledge, fist and arm hoisting me, one tug,
to the solid roof.

On the porch my mother stood silent, a dishrag
twisted in her hands, and I remember the expression
that passed from her face to his.
                              What did I do?
The rest of the day I sat on that porch
where I watched them move easily in the limbs of the oak
and felt on my wrist under the face of my watch
a sharp impression deepening to a bruise.

Appearances

Under a sky of stars and no moon, in the curve of headlights
alarming the county,
a line of deputies wades through a field
of waist-high hay. By a wall of gray pine at the edge
of that field, something curls, glows
bright as blood.
                    I curl under my blanket,
watch the yellow dial on the radio, the stars hanging
in the black panes of the window. This is real,
not make-believe horror, metallic, alive,
ultimately alien,

and the deputies trailing paths in the hay
move toward it, inch by inch, as the voice of the reporter
rises bodiless in my room, wind in his microphone
like a siren whistling the end of the world
as we know it. And I remember, vaguely, a night
my father carried me into,
a sky of loud crickets, a field of stars, a radio tower,
and circling the red light of that tower, two unknown lights,
balls of blue and green.

What those deputies find at the end of that field,
a piece of broken sign,
the letter O in fluorescent red, is nothing to ease my sleep.
I dream of the whole universe, of an infinite
and indiscriminate creation
where the black frontier behind the eyes floats back as far
as the light behind the stars.

Wings

What was it she taught
that the whole room had to be haunted by birds?

That night the telephone rang.
A crow on the mountain needs her wings clipped.
Why wasn't a question they thought to ask
when they gathered, four of them,
in the layered dark under the pine branches
on the hill overlooking the colored school.

The first one down kicked the latch, and the door
swung back. They closed it behind them
and felt through the room, wedging
into chairs, catching the moonlight that fell
through the windows. Which wasn't much,
but enough to see a buzzard
spreading black wings over a bookcase.
What in the world, one of them said,
then stood up and struck a match. A red bird
glared from a wall perch, then a jay,
a martin, a robin. A sparrow hawk
climbed the wall, talons balled on dusty fur.
When the match went out, a story
went around of a gypsy who could change herself
into a hawk. All across the county, not a hen
was safe. *I never heard such nonsense,*
someone said. Someone else struck a match
and held it in his face,
It's only a story, and shook it out.

Light rose like red smoke over the hill of pines
and flooded the window,
threw them all under the shadow of wings.
From the back of the room, a barn owl gazed
across a kingdom of birds, the mourning dove

flushed into the field of light,
the quail, the sparrow, the mockingbird,
all flying on strings under the blue ceiling.
Birds, someone said, and pointed a finger
like a gun. *Hush*,
outside, down the hill,
an engine, cylinders knocking like a bad heart.

They held their noise as the engine choked,
a door squeaked shut, light feet crossed cinders.
She stopped for a second on the stoop
while the broken latch rattled
on its hinge. Then wind swung the door, and all
through the schoolhouse
birds spooked under the wooden sky.

Good morning, she said, cool as the wind,
which didn't sit well with any of them.
In the wide-open door she stood, frail,
thin as a twig, and stared at the top of her desk.
Come to chop us some wood?

What was it she taught
in her school that a man could be haunted by wings,
could see one crow on a fence,
a grackle, the shadow
of a hawk, and find his hand flying up to his eyes?

What charms did she study
that in their memory a hand hacked loose from a wrist
could flap across a desk and fly away?

The Window

On Allgood Road two miles off Georgia 41, you round a curve
canopied by pine
and the house leaps out of the trees to meet you.

Upstairs in the far right window she waited for us,
she rocked in the shadows
of the wide magnolia. After school, newly licensed
by the state, we came to her in pairs, in carloads
leaning into that curve, reckless
on spirits, our hearts thrown to her
by the physics of desire,
and swore, no matter what speed we tore from the wheels
of our fathers, we'd seen her
in the upstairs window, a blossom of magnolia
in her hair.
                    These affairs got quickly out of hand,
other boys from other schools following suit,
and soon signs were posted,
the shade pulled down on that room for good.
But we came anyway, at night, in caravans
to see her silhouette in the window, evidence enough.

How long did this go on? All spring and summer,
until one boy threw caution too far into that curve.
After that they sealed the window with mortar and brick,
the room itself the shadow of a crypt.

That was half my life ago, and I've not swerved since
into the wrong lane of any curve. Nor forgotten
that house, the thick wreath
of magnolia branches, the zodiac
of white blossoms surrounding the window, the presence
waiting in that room, patient and promiscuous.

In Louisiana

Fog solid on the pond, I went anyway on that first cool night
of fall, staggering downhill
through wet grass, arms full of tackle, a boat motor,
toward the fence to be climbed and the jon boat
stuck on the mud beach,
and made it over that fence and halfway to the water
before the one root I stumbled over flew up and struck me
just below the knee.

For a long time I saw nothing
in dreams, then there was my father wading in the swamp,
     fog
like breath around his waist, and his arms
reaching into that fog, into the water
it hovered over somewhere in Louisiana, among roots
and other things hidden,
bringing up in his hands a tail like a copperhead's
but arm-thick and long,
as he dragged up thrashing on the other end
no head of a snake, but the chest and head of a boy,
his fingers still tangled in a knot of roots.
Always I'll remember
that gaped mouth drooling sludge, those dull fish eyes
wide in the new light
like the stunned eyes of the dying.
                     And that boy's face
changing around them into all the faces
I've seen enter that border of fog, struggling, beyond
help, as they stare fish-blind into the light of hospitals,
into the sun darkening the lips of ditches
and soggy fields,
their dumb, stunned eyes already clouding,
looking for one root,
the corner of a bed sheet, anything in the world to clutch.

Naval Photograph: 25 October 1942:
What the Hand May Be Saying

Reports of a Japanese surface presence have brought them
    speeding
into Savo Sound,
false reports that won't be true for days.

So now at evening the fleet drops anchor, the crews relax,
the heat drifts west toward the war in Africa.

On the deck of the tender *Tangier*
a sailor focuses a camera on a foreground of water,
the cruiser *Atlanta*, and far back against the jungles of Savo
the hulks of Task Group 66.4.

A few on the cruiser notice him, but you can't tell
from their faces, too many shadows, too long a stretch
of grainy water. Still,
figures can be seen loafing on the bow, leaning
from the bridge, the machine gun platforms, even a sailor
clowning on a gun turret, barrel straight up between his legs.

And behind the shadow draped like armor across that stern,
my father is standing with the gunners
under turret number six, a shadow
in a wide cluster of shadows waving toward the *Tangier*.

Knowing their future, I imagine
some pulse in the nerves, primitive as radar, throbbing,
and exactly what the hand is saying, even he doesn't know.
He is only standing where the living and the dead
lean against the rail,
unsure who is who, and wave across the sound
toward the camera, toward us, for all of the reasons anyone
    waves.

The Anniversary

This is the night I come to my room,
a bottle of brandy, or whiskey, a glass,
and close the door on the rest of the house,
pull the shades, switch off the lights,
imagine a darkness just as it may have been.
I pull my chair to the middle of the room,
fall to it like a man with a mission,
and do not turn on the radio, the stereo,
as I might do on any other night,
but listen to the pines brush the house
with a sound like the bow of a ship
rising and falling through water.
Then I drink for the shakes and I get them
when I see again jarring the darkness
the terrible rising sun, the searchlight
of the *Hiei* stabbing across the sound,
and jolt in my chair as the turret slues,
guns already deafening the long light blind.
Look, there he is at the door of the turret
and then, God, the blast of the shell
kicks him right back out! Then, God...
what? For this is the night my father,
forehead shattered, side pierced, was thrown
for dead from the deck of the *Atlanta*,
toward a place that was not Guadalcanal
or Florida Island, drifted like a man dead
to the world ending around him, and was dead
to the arms of the sailors in the lifeboat,
dead as any drunk in any armchair
who trembles at the horror of his thoughts
and learns, as he learns every year
that the power in the blood to terrify
is sometimes the power of love. So moves
one knee trembling toward his desk,
stands on shaky legs and puts down his glass,

leans on the desk and opens the drawer,
feels for the small pearl-handled knife,
the sharpest blade of Japanese steel,
This is your blood in remembrance of you,
who died one night at sea and lived,
brings it to his face, brings it to his eye,
touches with the nervous point
the flesh of his forehead, an old scar.

The Desk

Under the fire escape, crouched, one knee in cinders,
I pulled the ball-peen hammer from my belt,
cracked a square of window pane,
the gummed latch, and swung the window,
crawled through that stone hole into the boiler room
of Canton Elementary School, once Canton High,
where my father served three extra years
as star halfback and sprinter.
Behind a flashlight's
cane of light, I climbed a staircase almost a ladder
and found a door. On the second nudge of my shoulder,
it broke into a hallway dark as history,
at whose end lay the classroom I had studied
over and over in the deep obsession of memory.

I swept that room with my light – an empty blackboard,
a metal table, a half-globe lying on the floor
like a punctured basketball – then followed
that beam across the rows of desks,
the various catalogs of lovers, the lists
of all those who would and would not do what,
until it stopped on the corner desk of the back row,
and I saw again, after many years the name
of my father, my name, carved deep into the oak top.

To gauge the depth I ran my finger across that scar,
and wondered at the dreams he must have lived
as his eyes ran back and forth
from the cinder yard below the window
to the empty practice field
to the blade of his pocket knife etching carefully
the long, angular lines of his name,
the dreams he must have laid out one behind another
like yard lines, in the dull, pre-practice afternoons
of geography and civics, before he ever dreamed

of Savo Sound or Guadalcanal.
                              In honor of dreams
I sank to my knees on the smooth, oiled floor,
and stood my flashlight on its end.
Half the yellow circle lit the underedge of the desk,
the other threw a half-moon on the ceiling,
and in that split light I tapped the hammer
easy up the overhang of the desk top. Nothing gave
but the walls' sharp echo, so I swung again,
and again harder, and harder still in half anger
rising to anger at the stubborn joint, losing all fear
of my first crime against the city, the county,
the state, whatever government claimed dominion,
until I had hammered up in the ringing dark
a salvo of crossfire, and on a frantic recoil glanced
the flashlight, the classroom spinning black
as a coma.
                 I've often pictured the face of the teacher
whose student first pointed to that topless desk,
the shock of a slow hand rising from the back row,
their eyes meeting over the question of absence.
I've wondered too if some low authority of the system
discovered that shattered window,
and finding no typewriters, no business machines,
no audiovisual gear missing, failed to account for it,
so let it pass as minor vandalism.
                                    I've heard nothing.
And rarely do I fret when I see that oak scar leaning
against my basement wall, though I wonder what it means
to own my father's name.

IV: Armored Hearts

Armored Hearts

I'd been awakened before by hammers cracking across the
    pond,
but who'd be building at dawn? On a Sunday?

And I remembered the ducks, a loggerhead
must have eaten another duck. So I rolled into my jeans
and walked out onto the porch. Then the crack again,
and I saw through the fog dusting the banks and the pond
a man on the far bank, my neighbor
in the branches of a tree, his pistol
pecking at the water, and just the right angle
to catch my house with a ricochet.

Whatever new threat I shouted
must have worked. That afternoon he took to traps,
baiting his hooks with livers and fish heads,
floating them under milk jugs. All evening
I watched from my porch as he labored in his boat, knotting
his lines, tying his bait, easing out the jugs
like a rope of pearls,
and learned how much he cared for those ducks –

and how he must have hated what killed them, the snappers
with their ugly armored hearts, who wallow
like turnips in the muck of the bottom, clinging
to their stony solitude,
who refuse to sun, hiding like lost
fears, rising when they're least expected
into a panic of wings. This is what I thought about
as I rowed in the dark from one jug to the next, stripping
the bait from his hooks.

Snake on the Etowah

Kicking through woods and fields, I'd spooked several
and once stepped on a coachwhip among gravestones,
at least one garter curled like a bow
under ivy in my yard.
Once I even woke on the hazy bank of a lake,
wiped dew from my eyes and found
on my ankle
a cottonmouth draped like a bootlace.

I thought I knew how beauty could poison
a moment with fear,
but wading that low river, feet wide on rocks –
my rod hung on the backswing, my jitterbug
snagged on the sun –
I felt something brush my thigh.
The bronze spoon of a copperhead drifted
between my legs.

Out came the little tongue reaching
in two directions,
the head following upriver,
following down, then a wide undulation of tail,
a buff and copper swish. The river eased
around it in a quivering V,
while inside my shudder
it slipped out –
spiny, cool, just below
the surface, sidling against the current.

In a Kitchen, Late

If you stumble in the night out of your room of sleep
and step barefoot into the hall,
if you cross the dining room of close shadows, going
by touch along the edge of the table, the back
of a chair, the sideboard,
and stand in the doorway to the rich dark
of the kitchen, you can hear
over your held breath
a small stirring around the dog bowls.
And if you make yourself a part of the room, ease
along the counter to the fridge, pour its cold light
gently on the floor,
there they are – glossy carapace and brown wings,
always chasing the edge of the shadow.

It's good to sit in the dark in the rocker by the window,
your feet on the cool linoleum, to snack
on chicken and gaze across the deck
at the lake falling away from your fence, the woods
you'd love to be a part of. A pure loneliness,
watching needles buff the window with a darkness
you feel somehow you miss.

And if you wait long enough, without rocking,
making yourself no presence in the room,
they'll bring back
in perfect innocence through the veins of the house
their own small portion
of the night – out of the baseboards
and heater vents, faithful
as your ugliest desire, a stir
like a breath in the hairs of your leg.

Cemetery Wings

Sometimes a bright swarm of pennies in the grass, or a gold
mushroom quivering in the heat, sometimes only
the grass of the cemetery
rolling to more grass, hidden, nothing –
the warning I remembered when I heard the scream,
turned, and saw him dancing
away from the mower, the cloud trailing him
to the corner of the terrace. He fell.

I ran across the hundred yards of valley
and found him on his back
in the shadow of a wall, breathing hard against
the fumes of the mower, the sun, the stings knotting
his face and arms,
and dug into his pocket for the bottle
he'd rattled at me,
the blue pills for allergy.

If he knew me, I couldn't tell. He only stared
over the terrace at the thin cloud lifting
around the faces of angels, his eyes
wrinkled toward a question,
as though puzzled
at being carried away by such small wings.

American Mystic

Out of some toasty leaf-burrow she wallows into the cold,
following what calls her across
the icy crust of creek and up the ridge to my yard,
and shows herself in moonlight near the edge
of the pines, a shabby bag of nerves.

Her pink nose reads the air. Wind blurs
the suburb with snow.

I watch from the darkened kitchen, wondering if I've placed
the dog food too near the window,
and lose her for a moment to the neighbor's shrubs.
Then around the gatepost
a white snout follows a sniff, red eyes
inquire. She enters the yard
to chow at my bowl.

Always I let her eat
before rapping the glass to watch her bluff – a hiss
at the window, a flash of teeth.
But when I rap harder, that hysterical feint – the flip
to her back, eyes slammed shut, skinny
tongue lolling in the snow.

I fade behind the stove and wait. Wind spirits
the maples, the stars
vivify. Up she jerks, hissing at a mop,
a bag of pea gravel, a wheelbarrow
tumbled under the hedge,
and backs out of the yard delivered and alert,
bare-toothed, edgy.

Sierra Bear

One morning in June above Yosemite Valley, John Muir
    learned
the "right manners of the wilderness."
Walking out to sketch from the top of North Dome,
he followed his borrowed St. Bernard
to the edge of a meadow
and encountered, he says, his "first Sierra bear."

I like to picture that study in nature – artist and dog
poised in amazement at the heavy muscling,
the cinnamon elegance of pelt.
So easy to imagine the bear's huge grace –
sharp snout nuzzling air,
the small ears
twitching – you can almost understand an urge
to watch him run.
                    Here I smile at the eyes
of the bear as Muir, recalling
a rumor of shyness, "made a rush on him,
throwing up my arms, and shouting,"

and at Muir himself wincing as we all have
at our rude behavior. "As he held his ground
in a fighting attitude,
my mistake was monstrously plain."

Confused bear cocked back on a haunch,
artist's blundering arms frozen toward embrace –
what pardon these moments become
when the bear wades off through the lilies and grass.

A Night, Near Berkeley Springs

"The light of the future eternal" sometimes breaks on a life,
as Henry Kyd Douglas believed it touched
Stonewall Jackson when he broke his order mid-sentence –
"No, no, let us cross over the river and rest
in the shade of the trees."

And it doesn't always flare at the end, nor only strike
great generals – as Douglas himself learned
one night in Virginia
when he bedded his troops in an open field behind
the cavalry pickets. It was cloudy,
but not cold for winter. "In the middle of the night
I felt moisture on my face, and covering myself
from head to foot in a blanket
I slept soundly." And imagine a suffocating
absence of dreams, of waking
"oppressed with heat," the unnatural weight of the dark
burying you in a second of fear.

But beyond it, the awe, the simple joy
of rising up and shaking off that half-foot of snow,
of seeing outstretched from your feet the whole white field
mounded with graves,
and one by one in the early light
the glazed mounds quivering awake, each hopeless soldier
sitting up, brushing off
a fine dust, astonished to be rising from a cloud.

Home Maintenance

Ruin, she says, is the natural order.

You think she means the gutters choked with rot and
        seedlings,
the roof losing shingles like leaves. You think
of the backyard grown to pokeweed and car parts,
the fish pond clotted with algae.

Then one night two policemen knock
on your door and show you your hands, swollen, bloody,
show you the battered plaster
of your bedroom wall. The neighbors have been
        complaining,
hold down the noise or they'll take you in.
This is silly, you've already been taken in.
For years, you tell them, she's lied about you
to your children.

This is the night you sit in the porch swing,
holding your hands in a bucket of ice.

A few cars rattle by
and drown the hum of the crickets.
The air smells like magnolia blossoms and rain.
In Tattnall Square Park
the shadows of magnolias have swallowed the tire swings,
under a streetlamp grass cracks the tennis court.

She comes to you again, a shadow in the flower bed.
You open a loose fist.
Even now her meaning slips through your fingers
as she raises a glove full of roses.

Warbler at Howell's Drive-In

You might come here now
to go birding, and wandering through the undergrowth, run
across the ticket booth smothered in briars.

Speaker posts lean out of the woods like rusty saplings,
you pause for your bearings.

Somewhere off in the thicket was the popcorn stand
where two dollars took you
through a double feature – *Sunset Boulevard,*
Whatever Happened to Baby Jane?
The place was already seedy
and running down, and who wouldn't wince
at the lives started here on a passion thin as film?

A whistle, and a yellow-throat springs to a branch.
Your hand gropes the camera.

That blue Thunderbird,
the '68 with the jacked-up shocks? That was you then.
What junkyard is it rusting into?

And this is you now, middle age and beyond.
Those hot screen kisses that steamed up windows,
that rocked backseats,
gone now in the smoke of a blown projector.
And Gloria Swanson, Bette Davis,
all those others
we dreamed to be like? Hermited
in some mansion, plotting withered comebacks

(you fumble
the *f*-stop, the empty branch sways),

or gone into briars, pine needles, air?

Chinese Dragons

What do we want to give each other as we park under the
    sign
of the Electric Dragon?
Mysterious, you say, a name
like some bizarre arrangement of stars, a tail
of fire crawling all the way from China.

And tonight, looking up through the windshield
of my truck, we know already
what they'll be, no need to study the walls
of patterns, the yellow parrots
climbing stalks of cane, the rosebuds
unfolding under the paws
of red leopards, the erotic fish.

Hum of the needle, and that pale moment
of no turning back –
your eyes cut from mine
to the blue hand pointing toward the chair.

And when you sit in that chair, your blouse draped
on one shoulder, I know what claws out
of the sky and into your arm, what
will claw into my calf
and ankle, is something more than legend.

In your eyes as he needles the fire –
our desire for permanence and the permanence
of our desire.

Barriers

When thunder woke me to the early dark, I lay awake
    listening
to the pines whip the house,
and remembered a story a woman once told
of her childhood in California,
how storms off the Pacific
would wake her at night, frighten
her into her parents' room.
Such comfort and warmth, she said,
in those drowsy voices, that crawling under the covers
into their private dark. Sometimes she slept
beside her mother, sometimes
her father. How they must have loved her, she said,
though they never let her sleep between them.

I am not a father, but I think about the love of fathers,
the sheet thrown back for the daughter, the rough hand
rejoining the hand of the mother.
And because of her story
I know more about the love a man can feel for a woman,
love not born of the self
or what the self gives the world.

These nights alone
when the country lies between us like a curse,
I like to picture lightning flaring through the curtains
of a bedroom, a young girl standing
at the foot of a bed.
I try to imagine in the white spark of the window
the small angel her father saw,
her white gown the pure light of her heart,
and write in my letters
how love fears
even the barrier of a blessing.

Last Nickel Ranch: Plains, Montana

In the living room of the trailer, the father of the woman
I love calls the family into a huddle.
Dinner is over, the charcoal is ash on the grill.
Through the kitchen window, I watch rain drifting
like a ghost across the Cabinet Mountains.
We're leaving now,
and it's time for prayer.

The family circles to a hug and calls me in,
and for a moment, silence. Wind shakes
the tin sheets roofing the deck, the lambs
bleat from the hill behind us.
I think of prayer
and the humility necessary for prayer.

Then a squall of feathers from the guinea coop,
and in the corral
the burros scuffle against the water trough.
Hands join hands, and I catch the eagle's shadow

slicing down the ridge, one dark
blade of muscle
beautiful for its singularity.

I know what I've valued.
Last night I heard a coyote howling off the ridge
and went to the window.
In the darkness behind the glass
I saw myself, and behind my eyes the stars flew
into the pines.

Paper Route, Northwest Montana

Halfway home to the warm trailer, I stopped on a ledge
above the Clark Fork. Clear sky
brightened a loose change of stars,
and far out, the valley opened a white hand.
No hurry, the rest
of the route easy, plowed roads,
a few dozen tubes in the wilderness.

I took a long piss over the rocks, the cold steam
rising at my feet,
and below me in the splintered river,
an ice floe
drifted like a barge. Across that floe
something paced white against white.

Then the barking, and I leaned toward the ledge –
high, broken yelps dragging
their echoes up the cliff. Wind shocked
my face – who glimpses
the dead without shuddering?

Downriver the floe slid into the trees.
Wind silenced the river.

Sometimes in loneliness, I claim it
a blessing or when conversation
turns toward beauty – that huge, white splinter
drifting across the valley,
and on the point
a stunned, white wolf.

Hard Easter, Northwest Montana

Shadows from the spruce woods slouch down the hill,
the windmill's crippled shadow
pierces the house, a blue fog spirits
the trees and the full moon
floods the empty corral. Near the dark edge
of a scream, I hunch toward the Tensor,
working at the window
on taxes. The bleak numbers blur.

On the hillside the burro watches the moon.
How saintly she seemed this morning, half-blind
and motherly, bearing
her little cross,
leading the sheep to pasture,
and saintly now, frozen against the hill
by whatever weaves
the treeline, heard or felt.

A loose tarp flaps across the firewood
as wind creaks the deck,
and steadily the ridge shadows turn
under the moon,
the windmill's shadow follows toward the barn.
Such a picture of peace –
burro and sheep
grazing knapweed in the late snow.

Already they've forgotten the lamb's torn lung,
the purple knot of bowels
on stained rock,
while in the mountains beyond downed fences,
muscles stretch and shudder, sharp eyes
open underground.

Elegy for a Trapper

Eighteen below in Plains, Montana,
snow pack hardened to silk, and I rode with my father-in-law
to feed a man's dogs,
a favor for a deacon out of town over Christmas.
We four-wheeled a logging road, heater
rattling, and circled his log house big as a hunting lodge,
his three-sided shed walled with traps,
and found those dogs staked out in a clearing –
lean, shy, whimpering on the ice.

Almost a year to the day, I heard
he'd backed through the railing of his second-floor deck
to lay open his head on a rock,
and remembered dragging the water barrel up that slope,
my own breath icing my beard, ears burning
with brittle yelps,
bone-snaps of chains cracking out of ice.

And when I learned he was dead on arrival
at what passed for a local hospital,
I tried to find his wife in the log house,
and the nine-year-old
who must have shot baskets at the rusty hoop
nailed to the horse trailer,
but saw outside my window, in the afternoon blur
off the roof of Bank South, only
those hounds – two Walkers and a Blue –
and the hide of a coyote
draped on a tailgate,
a skinned bobcat, glassy, pink,
frozen upright on a stump.

Last Supper in Montana

My father-in-law begins the feast
by reading a few verses from the Gospel of Matthew,
then closes the book and lays it on the mantel.
With awkward solemnity
he breaks the body into thumbnails
and passes the plate among us, pours the blood
into plastic pill cups
his wife, a nurse, has rummaged from the clinic.

I swallow, and glance at my palm, the tangle of veins
in my wrist. A minute drips into an empty pan,
then a guinea screeches from the barn.
Prayer breaks out on the sofa,
and finally I see how a wound could bleed
for centuries, could trickle enough
to fill this cup.
                    Years ago, after my divorce,
I looked for my own way of renouncing
the world. I sat down in my kitchen and scratched
a list on a grocery bag,
every desire inked
in red, then carried a shovel into a grove,
wadded the bag and buried it.

But that was Florida, smothering heat,
bouts of booze and fever,
so what can I say for sure about surrender
or that lightness of heart?
                        Only that something
left me, and the wind knocked me down.
I don't remember what I felt like –
something small in the violence –
but I sprawled on my back

across that grave, clutching the wet grass,
and the oranges
kept flying through the leaves.

The Pentecostal

A few miles north of Thompson Falls, where the newspaper
    tubes
lean only occasionally out of the wilderness,
my father-in-law saw Christ walking
along the shoulder of the road. It was an icy night,
large stars over the old snow, the kind of weather
when the headlights of his truck
turned road gravel into precious jewels.
He would've been tired then too, only a few rolled papers
on the seat and the route taking him halfway to Glacier,
the window going up and down, the wind numbing
him through his coat. Singing
might've kept him awake, but he was praying aloud,
as he often does, when that something in the distance
crossed the edge of his lights.

That morning when he came home stunned,
he kept saying to his wife, *those eyes, those sad eyes,*
and it was an hour before she'd pieced the whole story.
He'd stagger against the kitchen counter, spilling
his coffee, weeping. *Those eyes,* he'd say,
the saddest eyes, which recalled for her their only son,
sixteen and curled behind the sofa, guarding
his ribs, cursing the boots and verses.
And years after that, those bloodshot eyes
in the patrol car window,
the eyes of their child evangelical,
their twelve-year-old witness, their runaway daughter.

The Blue Mountains

When a deacon in their church dreamt God would burn
    Portland,
my wife's niece and her German husband
packed everything they could into a Plymouth van.
It was one of those Sodom-and-Gomorrah things
and they were seventeen and twenty,
with a two-year-old son.

A hundred miles north there was a poor motel
and behind it a bony lake sprawling between mountains.
Twin beds, a shower, a pay phone
outside the office.
The news came in on a black and white Philco.

Portland had fires, of course –
a tanker flipped on the interstate,
a drunk on the west side fell asleep smoking.
But at the end of the week,
their money spent, their jobs in the wind,
the city was spared.

Mostly now they talk about the owls,
and the jostle of the boat as they rowed the lake,
the little wind, the pinched stars and the closing dark.
There were leaping trout too
and the baby crying to stand in the boat,
but mostly it's the owls, great horned or gray, heralding
those narrow passes,
bright as trumpets, far and farther.

Free Grace at Rose Hill

My uncle found it in a crater on Bloody Ridge
and stepped off a troop ship into Riverdale Baptist.
I heard it off his tongue
crackling like an open fire,
Love is fire. And once in remote mountains
at the church of a cousin, I heard
that sizzle in a wooden box a man had thrust his hand into.
What came up writhing in his fist
coiled above him like a sequined halo.

This was all argument, proof. I listened
my whole boyhood
and my listening couldn't save me.

But maybe you've walked on a Sunday in your favorite
        woods
and heard through the shuffling of leaves
the distant rustle of tongues, the handclapping,
the stirring of feet,
or the single inspired voice singing over a thunder of fans,

and maybe, like me, you paused once in the dogwoods
at the edge of that churchyard
to hear the many tongues rendering into one
the promise of an old hymn
and felt yourself listening suddenly
with your heart.

No, that wasn't grace either,
though grace had been there –
Isn't it like this cemetery where the roses
quaking in their terraces are not the wind?
It swirls where it wants to swirl.
If it touches us,
it touches us.

Zion Hill

Those anguished salesmen of the Scriptures,
those traveling healers and prophets, the beautiful handlers
of serpents who lift their faith
out of cages, the shakers and rollers,
the speakers in tongues, the footwashers
with their sweet pails of water,
all beckon again from their riverbanks and pine pulpits,
from the steamy fronts
of revival tents yellowed by lanterns.
And if I don't rise from my living room sofa
and drive all night to Zion Hill
where, one by one, in a bend of the river,
the elect of my family drenched themselves to the soul,
if I don't mail my check for a prayer rug, or lay
both hands on the radio,
it's not because I'm someone
who wants to be unremembered in his troubles,
or considers himself a physician
equal to his own heart.
Those oaks cooling that little field
of graves, the shingled arbor
under the cross, who could ever stop desiring
that serenity? Even if it's less out of devotion
than despair – the way a man
grown bald and sane in mid-management
will line his pocket with lottery tickets,
or dream through lunch of his resignation,
of barging into the board room, letter in hand,
smiling over his inheritance.

Horseshoes

Half my childhood my father carried in his dusty pocket
a miniature on a key chain, warm as a penny
when you rubbed it with your thumb.
Real ones lined a neighbor's drive, an uncle's flower bed,
and above the door of my grandfather's grocery
a parade shoe hung heels up
to keep what luck he had from spilling.

Wherever I looked there were horseshoes –
silver buckles, copper bracelets,
and dozens of pony shoes on the tack room floor,
strewn among the nails
you could throw like darts. Sometimes my cousin
rubbed a horseshoe before a test,
or carried it to school in her book bag.
A pharmacist at the Rexall, a man
I feared, wore a bright one of diamonds
in the hairs of a finger.
Everyone then seemed to need luck.

In that, at least, we're all old-fashioned.
Just last year a woman in Montana
bought a horseshoe
from a blacksmith who'd hammered it into a heart.
She mailed it to my wife as a Valentine.
Every few weeks it jars me awake,
clanging on the back porch, among the wind chimes.

A Home Buyer

I was so glad to be living in my own house again,
glad for a few rooms to wander through, a place to sprawl
outside the gaze of landlords,
that I walked all night from room to room,
onto the deck, into the yard, exploring
my pond of ivy, shadows of maple and dogwood.
I settled, finally, in the striped chair of the study
as a blue daybreak leaked like bar light
through the curtains
and brought back a place in Billings, Montana.
My wife danced there once with a woman in khakis
and followed her across the parking lot,
smoking, dizzy in the dry wind, and sat down on a tailgate
to watch the clear stars circling the mountains.
That was happiness, confidence, like a saint
or a schoolgirl, or some cowboy off the ranch in Rygate
who's driven into town for a Legion Hall dance,
some slicked-up kid with scuffs on his boots,
smart enough and handsome, a hard worker
who believes in virtue,
and knows the value of a dependable truck.

Sleepless Nights

One night, wasted, I went back and climbed the fence,
walked around the yard, pretending
to mow the grass. I sang old songs, got loud,
then afraid, and fell down
under the willow beside the pond.
The rock I'd fished off was there,
and the gouge in the bank where the boat slipped
onto those floating shadows.

In middle age you strike your bargain with shame,
and I leaned back against that tree, happy
and hurt to be trespassing.

Maybe she was out of town, or drunk herself
in a fast sleep, but no lights
came on, no policeman ever showed.
After a while the windows across the pond
went dark, and half a moon drifted
out of the pines.
              I knew I had to get up,
had to stagger back to my truck.
And that was my pain,
not in leaving that house or the water
or the sleeping woman, but simply
in that crawling up – broke
and exhausted, crawling up
without knowing what I'd fallen into,
or that I'd look back at myself
out of another night, pacing another darkness
ringed with geese and black sheep
and swans, singing again,
laughing, shouldering the complaints
of a newborn daughter.

A Daughter's Fever

Dark ivy draws a wave across the yard,
even the shadows
are streaked with rain. Light drizzles the oak leaves
and I rock behind this screen,
listening to squirrels, the bickering of jays.
The five a.m. garbage truck
doesn't wake you
as it scrapes the curb from can to can.
Three hours of crying lit the windows next door,
but now you lie as quiet
as the rain. After the dozen books,
the trail we frayed from piano
to puppets, to the cardboard frog
on his pond of cut wool,
I lean to your blanket
and hold my breath.

Rachel, about the little girl
who started home late
across the darkening woods…
Someday I'll give you the words I used all night
to guide her home. So many ways
to enter the forest and never return.
But happily that's another ending.

Under a basket of cornflowers
hung from the mantel,
she sleeps now in her cottage near the town.
Her father watches
new light clothe the trees.
In his orchard
the crows out-cackle the squirrels.
He holds his breath to hear
her breathe, around his finger
small fingers curl.

Shelves on the Clark Fork

I know you're restless,
the fields are drifting again into waxy shadows, waxy sky.
Still, I'm glad you've come
to keep me company under these fine stars and red moon,
especially here where the river sheds its trees
and all down the bank these stones recline
like a family sleeping.

This steam, aren't you tempted to call it breath?
The woman with the hunched shoulder, the grandfather,
the two young women, breast to back against the shelf –
maybe you knew them an eon ago.

What you ask here they answer in dreams.
Against that silence what argument is ambition?

Don't be upset. That's an owl, and farther off
a few sheep in an island of trees.
I love this wide sky – the distances between the stars
always increasing, the vacancy always increasing.

And why mind an owl, anything with wings?
Lie down for a moment, here
beside this child
curled around her mother's knee. Go ahead,
you can touch her, this is peace beyond violation.
Listen, you need to let go
of the people who have harmed you,
you need to slip out of those bruises
and across these stones.

My Perfect Night

First a tumble of clouds, muscular and black, full of noise,
then a star in a rift, remote
as a promise you intended to make. A moon, of course,
or half a moon battering those clouds with metallic light.
In my perfect night I hang this
over a clearing, a pasture, say, circled by woods.
Cows in their gentle bodies
sleep near the woods, black leaves float
and roll on the wind.
Far in the west, but not too far,
a few bears still dream
in the shadows of the foothills, a wolf eludes
extinction to lick dew off a stone.

In my perfect night I close the door on a dark house
and walk out into myself,
into the pines full of tree frogs. Somewhere in the dark
a cottonmouth flowers,
the carcass of a deer is lathered with flies.
In my perfect night I follow a trail by the river,
and my shadow on the water
looks deep and alive.

Allatoona Evening

Half a mile through a briar scrub thickening to woods,
I've lugged it like a sack of stones
and come to these shadows opening the cove.
A jon boat waits among the water lilies,
restless as wind, a paddle
in the bow, as though night were a current
to be muscled through.

On the horizon
a red glaze still treads water,
and in my silence, crickets choir the treeline.
Wave after wave, they call me to lay down
my anger. And the tree frogs
with them, barking out of the needles,
the copperhead skirting rushes,
sidling into the shallows –
lay it down, they say, on the green stones
beside this water.

A whippoorwill, an echo,
and above the drooping shoulders of the willows
delicate bats tumbling for flies –
lay it down, they say, your ambition,
which is only anger,
which sated could bring you to no better place.
Nothing is more beautiful than your emptiness,
and over the lake
these three stars soaking up twilight.

Notes

"Wrestling Angels" is for J. and Diana Stege, "Coasting Toward Midnight at the Southeastern Fair" for James Seay, "In Jimmy's Grill" for Gerald Duff, "Rubbing the Faces of Angels" for Lynn Jones, "Wakulla: Chasing the Gator's Eye" and "Home Maintenance" for Steve Belew, "Ice" for Dave Smith, "Awake" for Barry Hannah, "Under the Vulture-Tree" for Mary Oliver, "Barriers" for Kelly Beard, "My Perfect Night" for Bob Hill, and "Free Grace at Rose Hill" for Martin Bresnick. "Zion Hill" is for Charlie Smith and follows the method of his poem "This Holy Enterprise."

DAVID BOTTOMS' first book, *Shooting Rats at the Bibb County Dump*, was chosen by Robert Penn Warren as winner of the 1979 Walt Whitman Award of the Academy of American Poets. His poems have appeared widely in magazines such as *The Atlantic*, *The New Yorker*, *Harper's*, *Poetry*, and *The Paris Review*, as well as in numerous anthologies. He is the author of two other books of poetry, *In a U-Haul North of Damascus* and *Under the Vulture-Tree*, as well as two novels, *Any Cold Jordan* and *Easter Weekend*. Among his other awards are the Levinson Prize, an Ingram-Merrill Award, and an Award in Literature from the American Academy and Institute of Arts and Letters. An avid guitarist and fisherman, he divides his time between Georgia and Montana.

Book design and composition by John D. Berry, using Aldus PageMaker 5.0 and a Macintosh iivx. The type is Scala, a humanist typeface with an open character shape designed by Martin Majoor. Scala was created in 1988 for the printed matter of the *Muziekcentrum Vredenburg* in Utrecht, in the Netherlands, and released by FontShop International in 1991 as part of the FontFont series of digital typefaces.

The new Copper Canyon Press logo is the Chinese character for poetry, and is pronounced *shi*. It is composed of two simple characters: the righthand character is the phonetic and means "temple" or "hall," while the lefthand character means "speech" or "word." The calligraphy is by Yim Tse, who teaches at the University of British Columbia.